volume 2

SUB
MISSIVES

candid interviews
with 15 real life
submissives

COMPILED & EDITED BY ROY TURNER

MAGNOLIA BOOKS

This first edition published by Magnolia Books
Copyright © Magnolia Books 2014
www.magnolia-books.com

This book contains material from Domina Magazine,
originally published by Domina Publishing.

Cover photograph: Dreamstime
Book design: Mosquitomedia

The information, stories and articles contained in this book are
the opinion of the individual authors based on their personal
observations and years of experience. Neither the authors or
publisher assume any liability whatsoever for the use of or inability
to use any or all information contained in this book. Use this
information at your own risk.

ISBN-13: 978-1505342062

ISBN-10: 1505342066

Contents

Legal material   2
About the writer   4
Introduction   5
Chapter 1: Hillary   7
Chapter 2: Diane   15
Chapter 3: Swan   19
Chapter 4: Iris   26
Chapter 5: Jane   28
Chapter 6: Bronwyn   33
Chapter 7: Lucy   39
Chapter 8: Patty   48
Chapter 9: Anne   52
Chapter 10: Imogen   57
Chapter 11: Shayala   66
Chapter 12: Elizabeth   76
Chapter 13: Jessica   80
Chapter 14: Randi   85
Chapter 15: Clare   88
Other books from Magnolia   93
Dominatrix (Vol 1) Sample:
Mistress Xena   94
Submissive (Vol 1) Samples:
Janesca   102
Lorraine   114
'Marquis de Sade:
The Man and His Age' Samples:
Fashion   125
The Erotic Literature   134

About the writer

Born in London in 1952, Roy Turner graduated from Middlesex University and Saint Martins School of Art. He studied sociology and anthropology and wrote several historical biographies based on his extensive travels around the world.

Roy Turner was best known as the founder and editor of the fetish magazine Domina. Earlier career re-incarnations included teaching, acting, painting and decorating, carpentry, window dressing and window cleaning. He also worked briefly in a Wild West Rodeo in Arizona and had a shot at bullfighting in Spain.

Sadly, Roy died in 2007 after a long battle with cancer, but his diligent research and unique insights into the sadomasochistic world live on.

Introduction

"Submissive Volume 2', adds to the largely well received and popular Volume 1 in exploring deeper than ever before the largely hidden world of the submissive and masochistic female. If you thought Volume 1 was good then you're be sure to check out this one out as well.

This eBook is an extremely candid and definitive record of the experiences of 15 lifestyle submissive females, it certainly isn't some 'Fifty Shades of Grey' or Nancy Friday fantasy-fest. These women 'walk the talk'; whether it be extreme role-play, slave training, pony-girl, enforced servitude and prostitution, abduction and kidnapping. Consequently, some of the experiences related here could be considered extremely shocking and genuinely disturbing. It's definitely not one for the faint hearted!

For many interviewees, the need for domination had its roots, not surprisingly, in childhood. An authoritarian, even brutal, father started a trend which they sought to recreate in future relationships, but other subjects found themselves instinctively drawn to it for reasons less explicable, certainly not out of diminished self-esteem or anything that obvious. In many of the stories told, the division between controlled and controller becomes blurred, in other words, the so-called submissive is actually directing the scenario. By far the most popular and powerful scenario for most women was the idea of being used by two or more men, total humiliation and degradation often being the key driver.

A submissive is rarely passive, but invariably an active participant in the action, often directing the scenario 'from below' and letting the dominant man or woman know exactly what she wants. As one slave-girl put it: "A woman will follow where she wants to be led".

Publisher's Note: This book contains explicit sexual content, graphic language, and situations that some readers may find objectionable. It is intended for an adult audience.

Chapter 1: Hillary

Age: 37, Beautician, living in Hornchurch, Essex, UK

I'm not stupid, I'm not exploited, I'm not a pushover and I'm not anybody's for the taking, okay? I just want to get that straight first of all. It's just that my thing is submitting to my lover. I identify myself as a submissive female in a sexual sense only, that's all. It turns me on to give up all control, to put myself totally in his hands and let him do whatever he wants to me. Sometimes he ties me up, sometimes he doesn't. Sometimes he hits me with a paddle or a flogger or a cane, and sometimes he just gets me to serve him when we're in a scene space. That might mean fetching drinks, or doing a bit of housework in nothing but a frilly pinny and high heels, or it might mean giving him a blow-job while he watches the television.

There are all kinds of things we get up to. And I enjoy every single one of them. Okay, sometimes there are things I don't actually enjoy in themselves, but what gets me off, what gets me hot, is knowing that I'm doing it because he's told me to. I'm doing it because I want to please my Master. Yes, I do call him Master when we're doing scenes. He calls me his slut or his pet, depending on what sort of mood he's in.

It took me a while to acknowledge that I really am a submissive woman, a fem-sub. I grew up with some feminist ideas and ideals. I was always arguing with men about a woman's right to her own life, to do what she wanted when she wanted and never to obey anybody just because they had a cock. I hold down a good job and I'm in charge of six people, so I certainly don't spend my days cringing in a corner or waiting on my hands and knees for my Master to take any notice of me. That sort of thing works fine in books or porn films, but in the real world there are bills to be paid. We don't live together because both of us like our own space, and there is no way I would want anyone to be financially responsible for me.

Like I said, I'm a woman in control of her own life, and I always have been. I used to tease my friends about waiting for their 'prince' to come, and said I would never be bothered with all that sort of thing. But every now and again, I would find myself having these fantasies about strong, powerful blokes, about being helpless and made to orgasm again and again and again. I was never one of those feminists who hated everything about sex or campaigned against porn, and I had quite a bit of good straight sex before I discovered the S&M scene.

There was one boyfriend I had who liked to hold my wrists above my head when we were fucking, and that used to make me come twice as hard. I don't know if he thought of himself as kinky, or if he was actually into SM and keeping it quiet so as not to scare me. We broke up before I ever found out. Oh, there was nothing heavy about it, we'd been knocking around together for six months and his ex-girlfriend came back from her year abroad and that was that.

A while later I got in with a crowd of girls who liked going to the bigger fetish clubs in London like Torture Garden and Submission, and I started going with them. We'd all get really done up in leather and PVC and corsets and stuff from Camden and have a brilliant time, but I never went near the dungeon if there was one at the club. I was a bit scared that someone would grab me, and though I think a part of me wanted someone to do that anyway, I wasn't prepared to risk it. Gradually, though, I got to talk to other people who were more into the scene than I was, and when my mates got bored with the clubs and moved on to something else, I carried on going, and I started going to a few different ones as well. Mostly the sort of stuff I saw there was blokes getting dominated by women, kissing their boots and being whipped and acting as footrests, things like that. Once or twice I'd get them coming up to me and asking if they could lick my boots or something, which always made me feel kind of weird.

I was talking to people in the clubs much more now, and they started explaining to me that, while there weren't that many women on the club scene, there were plenty of them around and it was no more demeaning or degrading than anything else consenting adults want to do. I felt I was lucky that I had made such good friends, because it meant that I could experiment with people without putting myself at risk. I mean, I knew a couple called Sam and Donna (not their real names, of course) and in public he was generally the sub, but actually they were both switches and, one time at this club, they tied me over the whipping stool and both of them had a go at me, which was really amazing. I was a bit shy and scared about it, but that turned me on even more and though I couldn't let go enough in the club, I got very trippy and high on the flogging and, when I got home I just had to wank myself off—immediately!

I started playing a bit more after that, always with mates, always with people I knew and trusted, and then I had my first fling as an 'outed' submissive woman with a guy I'll call Mike. We had a pretty good time together for nearly a year, going to clubs and parties and getting up to all sorts. He'd tie me up to a St. Andrew's cross in a club and go for me with a soft suede flogger, then flick my nipples with a riding crop, and once he dripped hot wax on my arse, let it dry, then whipped it off with a single-tailed whip, which was pretty damned horny, I can tell you. We got along reasonably well, but ultimately didn't have much in common apart from kinky sex, so we sort of drifted apart.

Of course, having tasted what it was like to be dominated by a man I fancied the pants off, I wanted to do it some more, so I started looking for a partner who could do all those terrific 'dirty' things to me. Once again, I was really glad of my scene mates, because they knew lots more people than I did and they had also taught me how to spot an arsehole a mile off. You do get a few fair blokes in this scene calling themselves dominants or 'tops' who are really just into pushing people around. I've heard one or two really nasty stories about guys who can't tell the difference between SM and domestic violence, guys who need psychiatric help or a prison sentence or both!

Never mind the dick heads who just want a house wife or sex slave and reckon they'll never have to lift a finger again. The whole point about SM and the sub/dom thing is that it works both ways, or should do. There has to be trust on both sides. I know there are some people who reckon that, once you've found your perfect partner then you should be Master or Mistress and slave all the time, 'life style' they call it, but I can't see the point of it myself. I mean, who the hell wants to walk around a supermarket in full rubber kit on a lead? You'd only get arrested or laughed at or even beaten-up! Okay, I have heard them talk about it a lot and I've met some couples where the sub is 'collared'; that is, they have a collar that they wear all the time to show that they belong to someone.

That's not really for me though. I do wear a collar sometimes when I'm playing a scene with my Master, but to us it's just something that we both like to wear at certain times. Some people do make a very big deal out of putting the collar on the slave. The whole idea is that it's like a wedding ring or something like that. Actually, I have been to a collaring ceremony with my Master and it was lovely. It was quite moving because it obviously meant a lot to the Mistress and her slave who were doing it. Like I said, though, it's not for me or my Master.

My collar is black PVC with a ring on the front, and I have worn it to go clubbing with him. Once or twice he has brought a lead with him, and I've been on the lead all night, which was quite fun. Yes, he lets me go off it when I need the toilet, or when he's sending me to the bar, but a lot of the time he'll be sitting down and I'll be kneeling on the floor beside him with him holding my lead. It makes me feel sort of irresponsible and totally safe at the same time. I don't have to think, I don't have to worry, I just have to obey.

This really isn't something I'd want to do all the time, as I keep saying. Of course it's not. I like to go to work and boss my staff around and get the job done. I like to treat myself to new shoes or cinema tickets or whatever. There's a whole world out there a lot bigger than the world of the dungeon, and I really don't get the mind set of those people who want to be chained up forever and totally owned. I don't actually think anyone really wants that.

You hear occasional stories of people who have managed to make themselves legally slave and master in all but name. The Master or Mistress has power of attorney over the slave's finances and they aren't allowed out of the house, but I never knew of one of those contracts that stood up. And I've never met anyone who really claims to have a slave in the basement who is entirely their property, and I think that most of the people who say they want that sort of thing are fantasising, really. My Master agrees and says he couldn't imagine a top or dominant wanting to take it that far. Besides everything else, it would be an awful lot of hassle and responsibility.

That's something a lot of people don't seem to get about the whole BDSM thing, that as a submissive you do have to take some sort of responsibility for yourself. When I said earlier that I like the way that scenes with my Master let me be and feel completely irresponsible, that's only applying to scene space, to when we're in an SM mind set and an SM situation, and I only let go like that with someone I know and trust very well. You do have to take some time to get to know someone before you hand over that much power to them; either that or you have to develop a good sound instinct about people.

Nowadays a lot of people are looking for slaves or masters over the Internet and, while there's nothing wrong with that, some of them seem to have got into this weird mind set where subs have got to be protected from themselves. I remember a big discussion about setting up a 'Dangerous Doms' list to make sure that none of us silly sub girlies got into anything we couldn't handle, and that made me furious. Like I said at the beginning, I may be submissive, but that doesn't mean I'm too stupid or pathetic not to be able to tell someone to fuck off, or to refuse to have anything to do with them if I didn't like them.

Having talked to a lot of people on the scene, I know that some subs of both genders have got themselves into trouble, but what some idiots seem to forget is that, just because someone calls themselves a submissive, doesn't mean they might not be big and physically strong enough to hurt or frighten a dominant partner who just happens to be smaller than they are. SM and sub/dom are not about who gets to be boss because they've won the right to it in an arm wrestling contest. Well, not unless that's your particular kink, I guess.

I met a sub girl once who'd been through all this shit with tops. Everyone had let her down and hurt her or misused her trust. I felt sorry for her at first until I got to know her. Basically, her big thing was being submissive to a heterosexual couple, or so she claimed. She'd get together with couples who switched or were both dominant, and then she'd end up messing them about, causing huge rows between them, then running off crying that yet another person had broken her heart! I got the impression that what she was really after was to take the bloke away from the woman each time, and when it didn't work it was, to her at least, because they were such terrible people. Mind you, I later met someone who had been involved with her and they didn't have much good to say about her.

The woman involved was a dom with a switch boyfriend, and they'd taken up with this girl for a few weeks. They said she was incredibly needy and pushing for way too much too fast. She wanted to be accepted as their slave and collared on about the second time they met her. And the thing was that neither of them wanted a full time slave or third party in their relationship anyway. They were happy enough to fool around with her and be friends, but she seemed to take everything too far and assume that they were going to commit to her completely without ever discussing it with them or asking them first.

You do get some subs who are obsessed with getting exactly what they want and don't give a toss about what a Master or Mistress needs. I've met a few, a lot of them sub men, who think that, just because I'm a girl, and not what you'd call petite and, if Master's not out with me, not obviously with anyone, that they can get me to dominate them. Never mind that I'm one hundred per cent submissive and have no interest in being a dominant. They just think that by outlining exactly what they want to anyone with a pair of tits, they will automatically get it and, if they don't, they start moaning on about how 'cliquey' everyone is. You never seem to be able to get them to see that SM is not a one-way thing.

We call it topping from the bottom, and no one likes it. I really try to submit properly when I'm with a Master. Oh dear, I can really just picture his face when he reads that bit. I think I might be in for a certain amount of tickle torture or something like that later on. No, I'm a good 'subbie' girl really, and I only spoke up without permission once when there was a bloody great spider lurking underneath the whipping bench and Master is even more scared of spiders than I am. I got an extra few spanks for it, just the same. At least he didn't order me to deal with the spider myself!

Another dom male I know reckons you can push people's limits, as he calls it, when they're in a submissive head space, and that way you can order a slave or sub to do something they absolutely hate. I've got my doubts about that sort of thing, where it starts tipping into abuse. It's like I said, to me being a submissive woman is about placing absolute trust in someone for the duration of the scene at least, which means I don't expect them to do anything that would really hurt or upset me. If you're in a relationship with someone who keeps making you do things that are dodgy or bad for you, then you might want to think again about that relationship.

I knew a girl once, or knew of her, I should say, as she left the scene soon after this, whose Master wouldn't let her speak to anyone or see anyone outside of the scene including her family. He got her to leave her job and get another one with a friend of his. She wasn't allowed any money or to even use the phone without permission. Of course, he also took to beating her in a way that wasn't SM at all. Finally she managed to tell someone in a club what was happening and everyone rallied around and got her away from the arse hole.

It isn't that I think being a Master or Mistress is always likely to tip over into abuse. I know damn well that my Master won't abuse me. I did have a lot of struggles with myself about acknowledging my submissive streak, and I can understand why a lot of people worry more about submissive women than they do about men, because of the whole social legacy of women being men's property and having to submit whether they liked it or not. I just think that some people are sexually submissive, whether they are men or women, gay or straight, and they are going to be happiest when they acknowledge that and go out and find people that they can share that with.

Being a submissive doesn't make you a wimp or a traitor to your sex or anything like that. It's a matter of knowing yourself and what you want, taking responsibility for yourself and your choices, and living the life you choose to live. And I think that takes guts and grace, and I will never let anyone make me ashamed of my desires or my choices in life.

Chapter 2: Diane

Age: 37, Fashion Designer, living in Brighton, Sussex, UK

We are pretty unique as a sub/dom couple I would imagine as both Mike and I are quite into the 'sub' bit more than the dom aspect. All the couples I know or have heard about work on the principle of one being dominant and the other being submissive. I'm just talking sexually here. In our ordinary life we are, well, quite normal really. But in a sexual context I'm usually the dominant partner, except when our fantasies extend into threesomes and group scenes. Then we found we are both turned on by the idea of being used by dominant males.

In case you're confused by all these variables I'd better just explain at this point that my partner is a bisexual transvestite. I knew this about him right from the start of our relationship and it was, in fact, a big part of the initial attraction. You'd be amazed at the avenues of erotic exploration this can open up. For instance, we can be male and female lovers, other times lesbians. Our biggest fantasy, and one that we have turned into reality on occasion, is that we both share the same guy. Sometimes this is as sluttish girls and sometimes with him retaining his male persona.

As two submissive sluts we have to serve our master in any way he desires. We love kneeling together and sucking on the same guys cock and, after he's ejaculated, we pass the spunk between our mouths as we kiss. Only occasionally have we engaged in group sex with lots of men and that was with a group of bisexual men who hold a weekly party in a private house in London. They don't usually encourage females to their get-togethers because, apparently, females even at swinger type parties tend to be monogamous. They will pick one guy they like and stay with him for the whole evening, ignoring all the other men present. This kind of behaviour understandably pisses off the rest of the men. They let me come along because I've always enjoyed taking on groups of guys and I was a regular swinger long before I met Mike.

The people who attend these small gatherings all know each other very well and understand where we are coming from and are quite happy to play along with our games. As females, me and Mike, or Michelle as he is known en femme, love to be used by anyone who wants to have us. We both like receiving anal sex and really enjoy being placed doggy-style facing each other so we can watch one anothers pleasure.

A favourite fantasy, and one that is unlikely to come about, is one where we are having sex in some woods and get discovered by a patrol of soldiers. Apparently, we are on their gunnery range or something like that. The soldiers take us prisoner. We're still stark naked, of course. Coincidentally, and happily for us, all the soldiers turn out to bisexual. I did tell you this was pretty hard to achieve in real life stuff, didn't I? Anyway, we are both pored over and groped while being held at gun point. They notice Mike is getting an erection while having his balls fondled by a big, burly sergeant. They smile approvingly at this, realising that his arousal must mean he is one of them, and start getting out their own cocks and wanking.

I am held tight by two soldiers who are fingering my pussy and ass-hole. The rest drop their pants and bend Mike over a fallen tree and gang bang him while I am forced to watch. When they're finished they turn their attentions to me and give me the same treatment while Mike is this time forced to watch me being ravished. Variations on this fantasy include being used by Hells Angels or African rebels.

One of the most exciting experiences we've had in this scene is to meet and play with a dominant married couple. They were both bisexual as we are and were equally delighted to meet a submissive couple. There are so many erotic variations and permutations in this combination that it would take ages to tell you about them all. And we're still exploring!

Both Michelle and I are very into playing the role of maid, for instance. We've already served our dominant friends at their parties and, of course, been punished and used by all their friends. They also have a proper dungeon too, which we lack ourselves. This makes the scene life a lot more interesting. We have the long wait and all that anticipation for our punishment, tied up naked side by side. Sometimes they will just use me sexually and leave Michelle tied in torment, unable to do anything but watch me get a good sorting out.

Another variation we've enjoyed when playing with single dominant males is where we have a three-tier hierarchy. In this game I am subservient to the Master, but dominant to Mike. I love fucking guys in front of him and letting him know how good a fuck they are. One guy in particular, who we trust implicitly to appreciate the boundaries of play, we even invite over to spend the whole weekend with us. Mike is forced out of our bed and only allowed to sleep in a sort of dog basket thing at the foot of the bed. If he's good he's allowed to watch us fuck. But if he's bad then he has to be blind folded and only allowed to hear us make love and imagine what's going on. He'll also have to serve us in his maid's uniform.

You can only achieve this level of role play with someone you trust implicitly. I would recommend that couples who are keen to experiment as we do should be very, very careful about choosing their playmates. There's no getting away from the hard fact that this is a very dangerous game to play and I've seen couples get into a lot of trouble and come very unstuck. They think they can handle it, but they can't really.

One couple we know of, in particular, had their marriage completely destroyed by it. Admittedly, this was a bit different as she was a professional dominatrix who ran off with one of her slaves after getting pregnant by him. Although their situation was a long way from ours, the principle is still the same. Be very, very careful. Having said that, the plus points do make it worth the risks involved.

When it works well, it is the most exciting and fulfilling experience. I feel we have grown together as a couple much more than so-called straight couples. After all, how many husbands and wives do you know who discuss their tastes in men and swap skirts?

Chapter 3: Swan

Age: 48, Ophthalmologist living in Humberside, UK

You asked me what dangerous things I have done in my pursuit of the perfect master. In one of my ads in a sex contact magazine I received a letter from a man whose ideas excited me very much. So I answered, telling him briefly what I was looking for. He replied with a photo. But he was too old for me and I didn't find him at all attractive. I wrote back and made some excuse, but he wouldn't let it go. In the end I spoke to him on the telephone and tried to explain how I felt. He was obviously offended. He suggested that if I liked his ideas it didn't really matter if I found him old and unattractive. If I was blindfolded, he said, it wouldn't make any difference anyway.

After much deliberation I turned up at his house, which was two hours drive from my home. The front door was on the latch, as he said it would be, so I let myself into the hall. There I blindfolded and handcuffed myself as he had instructed and awaited his appearance. After five minutes of exquisite suspense I heard his footsteps approaching and felt his hands stripping me, then examining me intimately. I was then led upstairs, tied tightly spread-eagled to a bed and gagged. He then went on to introduce me to the slow, teasing, excruciating joys of pleasure and pain. He had me bound in so many places and so open I could do nothing. The gag was a tight head harness that ruled out any communication. This was my first experience and I was so incredibly turned on I thought I would faint.

My knees were drawn tightly outwards, as were my thighs, so

my cunt was completely unprotected. After hours of exquisite torture (during which time I had soaked the bed with my juices) he inserted one solitary finger up my cunt. Up until then, even though I had writhed and begged, he had not penetrated me at all. This one finger was like giving someone dying of thirst a tiny drop of water. He set up a rhythm of very slow penetration then withdrawal. The movement was so slow I never knew if each thrust were the last. Each time his finger was deep inside me his knuckle brushed my clitoris.

I smelt him light a candle with his other hand. I was petrified but could do nothing about it. I was completely in his power. He dripped hot wax over my bound and aching breasts and nipples, still keeping up the rhythm with his finger all the while. As the wax travelled down my torso, his other hand slid up the dripping gap of my cunt and slipped the fleshy hood back to expose my very vulnerable and very hard clitoris. A second finger was inserted. The penetration was still very slow, but at least it was now deeper. By this stage I was slobbering like an animal. I would have done anything to achieve the sheer relief of orgasm!

The wax had reached my pubic hair when I realised what he was going to do next. I can't describe in words how I felt, but I think demented comes close! He held my clitoral hood back and dripped one exquisite drop of excruciating wax. It gave me the most amazing orgasm imaginable and was the only time I ever came without manual stimulation of some kind.

I left without ever seeing him and never went back. But the experience obviously had a profound effect on me. I think I have been striving for its equal ever since.

That first experience fired my imagination to seek out other dangerous liaisons. Another guy I met on a chat line was very dominant and we had many very horny conversations over several months. We were both turned on by the idea of completely anonymous sex. So, in the end it culminated with a most amazing and daring meeting. I know people will think I'm completely mad when I tell you that I invited this guy I'd never clapped eyes on to come to my house and use me. The scenario we worked out was that he would show up at my house at a given time. I would be stark naked and lying on the bed after leaving the front door ajar so he could let himself in and come straight up to the bedroom and fuck me.

More than anything I would like to be tied to a hard backed chair with my legs spread apart so I can't even grip my thighs together to relieve the pressure. After giving me a firm instruction not to move, my master torments and teases me until I am at boiling point. Then, when I have pleaded long enough, he undoes his trousers. They sit on his waist, but I can see the bulge of his cock through the gap. He steps out of sight behind the chair and rests his hard-on into the my tied and cupped hands. Then he reaches in front of me and grasps my nipples. At the same time he tells me once more I am not allowed to move my hands to caress him. The thought of his pulsating cock drives me crazy. Nothing, not even the threat of pain and punishment is enough to stop me caressing his thick, hard shaft with my bound hands. I imagine how it would be to watch him slowly masturbate himself in front of me.

He then removes his clothes and sits his balls in my cupped hands. He squeezes my nipples very hard, reminding me yet again of his order not to move. I'm so excited, I ignore his instructions for as long as I can withstand the pain just for the pleasure of holding him and feeling his rampant cock in my hand. All the while he makes me pay for the pleasure by increasing the punishment until I am in so much pain and frustration I could scream. Then he walks in front of me at last. He is naked and I can now see his erection, all purple and hard. He stands between my knees, takes his cock in his hand and very slowly masturbates all over my bound breasts which are, by this time, boiling and bright red from the punishment he has meted out.

Next, he releases me and orders me onto the floor on all fours. My breasts are still glistening from his spunk. He orders me to stretch my arms out in front of me until my head is on the floor. This has the effect of raising my buttocks into the air. My master makes me spread my knees as far apart as possible by slapping the inside of my thighs until he is satisfied that I can spread them no further. He then tells me that he intends to test my reactions to different stimuli on, in and around my two orifices. He also intends finding out how tough a spanking I can take on my backside and cunt. And finally, that he intends penetrating me. First annally with one finger. Then with additional fingers until I am so full I beg him to stop. But would he stop, even if I begged?

Between each test of my obedience and acceptance he rewards me with his mouth and tongue. However, even for my reward, I have to endure the sweet humiliation of holding my own bottom cheeks apart to expose my asshole to his gaze. At first I balk at the idea of opening myself so intimately for his administrations. But he strokes my bottom so sensuously with the palm of his hand and cajoles me, telling me what a good girl I am and that I must obey or he will be forced to punish me.

I feel my sphincter muscles contract at the thought of the invasion to come. He insists that I must relax and allow him entry or I will regret it. As encouragement, his hot tongue probes and licks my asshole until I am reduced to a hole for his use, to do with as he will. I can resist no longer and my bowels turn to jelly as I give myself to him.

He repeats the process with my cunt and fills both holes simultaneously. I am grunting and pleading and riding his hands like a demented animal. All the time he is telling me what a dirty bitch I am, and what he can see and how exposed I am. I finally come when he informs me: 'When I have finished with you, you will allow me to do anything I like without question. You will obey me with out even thinking. Is that clear.'

Each time I have this fantasy, I usually end up mumbling "yes" into my pillow.

Being spanked has always been a fantasy of mine, but I haven't yet found a man who wants to spank me as much as I want to be spanked. It's strange, too, that in my fantasies I extend things further than I would accept in real life. I think I would need quite a lot of pleasure combined with the pain in order to endure the levels of spankings I dream about! I'm not sure if I could bring myself to ask for it. Basically, it's all a grey area for me, apart from in my fantasy. I would need a man who is prepared to start from square one and help me explore the humiliation, as well as the pleasure and the pain.

My spanking fantasies sometimes incorporate a schoolgirl scenario. The 'teacher' of my dreams is a slightly shadowy figure in a traditional gown and mortar board standing by the side of a large oak desk in a book lined study. He is standing with his feet apart and hands clasped behind his back when I knock and enter. He is a very imposing, authoritative sight and me, in my school uniform and white 'virgin' socks, am naturally very intimidated at having to face him.

My punishment consists of me being told to lie across the desk. The edge of the desk is in my groin and my legs over the side. The desk is so tall my plimsolled feet don't quite touch the floor, so the teacher has to tie my ankle to the legs of the desk. With very experienced hands he lowers my school knickers until they are stretched across my thighs. My hands grip the other side of the desk, the knuckles white with tension. My face is crushed against the hard wood desk and strained with arousal between my outstretched arms. Because my ankles are tied to the desk legs, my thighs are parted and showing a glimpse of my parted sex lips, all swollen with need.

The slight glimpse of my sex surrounded by the expanse of spankable flesh arouses the teacher as he administers my punishment. Somehow I know I have caused 'Sir' to have a terrific erection! He cannot resist accidentally probing me and, eventually, discovers my own shameless arousal. Of course, this provokes further examinations and the inevitable humiliating exclamations of disgust at my wantonness!

In my fantasy, after the exquisite round of punishment and humiliation that has left my buttocks and thighs hot and throbbing and scarlet, I would be ordered to remove my knickers completely. They would then be stuffed in my mouth and held in place by a leather belt. On instruction I would scramble across the hard, unyielding lap of my teacher and spread my legs as wide as possible. I can feel teacher's erect cock throbbing against my belly. His hands on my lower back hold my wrists in place. They should be strong and firm, but restrained to show his absolute control over me. Heaven!

The spankings would then continue, but this time would also include blows aimed specifically at my shamelessly dribbling cunt. When he has finally reduced me to a snivelling heap, he would grasp my hair and pull me off his lap, forcing me to kneel between his legs. Removing my knicker-gag he will unbutton his trousers and pull out his very big and very hard cock. Waving it accusingly in my face he would admonish me sternly for causing something like that to happen with my sluttish behaviour.

'What do you intend to do about it, young lady?' he demands menacingly.

'I don't know, sir.' I answer with a meek and quaking little-girl voice.

'I think you do, my girl.' He says as he grips the back of my head with his large hand and guides my hungry mouth toward his monstrous erection. Like a mad thing I gobble on his cock until I can feel him building up to the point of no return. At the last moment he withdraws his cock from my mouth and orders me to hand him my knickers which are now lying discarded on the floor.

He then proceeds to shoot his entire load into my school panties! I watch mesmerised as jet after jet of white cum soaks my underwear. When he's finished he wipes himself off on my knickers and tells me to put them back on. I am then dismissed and forced to spend the rest of the day sitting in class with a hot bottom and spunk sodden underwear to remind me of the whore I am!

I am very aroused whenever I read about spanking or bondage. I think I must be very unsure of my level of need however because, even though my heart races at the thought of being in the hands of a dominant man who knows what spanking is all about, I immediately get worried that I am encouraging him to think the wrong things. For all I know spanking to him might mean nothing else, just constant pain until I am sobbing and begging him to stop. Bondage, too, might mean nothing more than binding me tightly and leaving me for hours with no stimulation apart from the cut of the ropes. I know there are some people who 'get off' sexually on pain alone, but I'm afraid I don't fall into that category. I only enjoy bondage if it is to make me available for sex. And spanking can only be as hard as the pleasure overriding it.

Now that I have made that clear I can tell you that I do fantasise at length and in great detail about being 'firmly prodded' into exceeding my limits, not only of pain, but of what is 'acceptable' i.e. size, duration, pain level, pleasure level, humiliation level. But I have yet to meet a man who doesn't need to be told how to 'persuade' me, by fair means or foul, to exceed my limits.

I love bondage too, as I've said, but recently I have found my thoughts turning to a 'new toy'. I had a very brief taste of 'mental restraint' and found it thrilling i.e. the master tells me to stand still and accept whatever he is going to do to me. I will not be allowed to shut my legs or take my hands off my head until he has finished. If I do he will punish me. Then I am made to accept more pain than I would choose (slightly!) or penetration that again stretches my limits. If I do move my legs or disobey orders, then the punishment is real, thereby forcing me to extend my limits. I'm not sure if I explained that very well, but I'm sure you got the gist of it.

I find that my levels of involvement in the darker side of my sexuality leave anyone else I've met trailing behind. I am like a student thirsty for knowledge. I am petrified at the thoughts that go through my head sometimes and also by the amazing acts that I now find totally acceptable but would have been horrified at five years ago. Sometimes I am convinced that with the right man I could live as a sex-slave and want for nothing more. Then I would probably just spend weeks craving straight sex just to prove I can still be aroused by it and that I don't need orders to follow to be able to enjoy sex. See how confused I am? I want more, but more scares me to hell! All I know is that I have a craving inside me that eats away at my soul but remains forever elusive.

Chapter 4: Iris

Age: 50, Former Croupier, living in Suffolk, UK

I don't have any time for people in the so-called fetish scene. As far as I'm concerned all they are interested in is dressing up and playing their silly little sex games with each other. What they do is simple role play. It's fantasy, pure and simple. Like children dressing up as cowboys and Indians or doctors and nurses. What I do is real and it is my whole life and what I live for. I was born to be a slave. I have always known this was my destiny and I have paid the price for this destiny by being wrongly sectioned in mental institutions on more than one occasion. Because I choose to live a life that is beyond the understanding of most people, society decides you are insane. It is the only way they can deal with you on their terms.

The first time I was sectioned happened to me after my period of abduction in the mid-eighties, which the police still refuse to believe happened to me. But, then again, I have my own theories about that, which I will explain to you as much as I can. You have to understand there are a lot of things I can't tell you because the men who enslaved me are very powerful. More powerful than you can imagine. What I can reveal is that I was approached via an advert of mine in a contact magazine by a man who turned out to be a member of an international society of dominant masters. He was a middle eastern master and was visiting London for the express purpose of procuring female slaves. We arranged to meet at his central London hotel. When I arrived I found he had a whole suite to himself and was obviously very rich.

The interview lasted several hours during which time he asked very deep and perceptive questions to determine I was truly slave material and not one of these silly women who just want to play at sub/dom. He also put me through a series of physical tests of pain and endurance and humiliation to further determine my aptitude. These he called 'challenges'. When he was satisfied I was suitable slave material he informed me that I would be 'exported' to his home country to live as a full-time slave.

He gave me one last chance to decide if this was really what I wanted. He said this would be the last decision I would ever have to make in my life. If I decided I didn't want this, I could leave the room and go home and resume my old life. I would not be contacted again. If, on the other hand, I agreed to accept, my life would change from that very moment. I felt this was the moment I had been waiting for all my life and had no hesitation in saying yes. That was the last thing I remembered. Later I learned that I had been drugged and shipped to the middle east in a crate marked livestock. The men in the society can do this quite easily because they have diplomatic immunity.

I know all this sounds far fetched but it is all true. In fact, it happens all the time. What do you think happens to all these young women and girls who disappear? You read about it all the time in the newspapers, don't you? Do you really think they have all been murdered? Of course not, no one questions it. Even when they find a body, are you really sure they have? This society has strong connections with the police, you know, as I hinted at before. I can't say too much or I will put my life at risk, but they can do pretty much what they want. The parents of the missing or 'allegedly' murdered girls are either in the society themselves or are paid a considerable sum of money to allow their daughters to be taken as sex slaves. That's why I was put into mental hospitals. They wanted to silence me and the best way to do it is to pretend I am mad. They simply can't afford to have someone like me telling the truth about them.

Chapter 5: Jane

Age: 43, Writer, living in White Plains, USA

People keep telling me I'm naturally dominant, but I'm not! Nothing gets me more than the thought of sweet submission, humiliation and control. I just need a worthy master with some intelligence to make me flower into full bloom. Sex is what drives me. It powers most of my life, running through everything I do. It powers my mind, without it I shrink and begin to curl up inside.

I need this 'mind feeding' to be able to be confident in sex; that's why I believe I'm naturally submissive. I need to shine in someone else's light and get brighter. I need someone else to 'be for'. But because I'm a strong character, it's not easy to find someone confident enough in themselves to take control over me. Lesser masters use brutality and bullying to gain it. I would never give control. It would have to be cleverly taken, and they would have to be convinced I was worth the effort. And I would have to believe beyond any doubt that I couldn't get the better of them.

All my lovers are gods to me, and if I find I can run rings round them I lose respect for them straight away. They become mere mortals like all the rest and, like a darkened angel, they fall from grace. I realise, even as I write, that this isn't a very 'submissive' thing to say at all, is it? But, there in, lies my complexities and my problems and my mystery!

I discovered the delights of perversion quite recently, but the confines of my life makes it hard for me to chase her pleasures. She

throws all kinds of practical obstacles in my way, tripping me at each new turn of my chosen path. So a master must bear that in mind when he entices me. He will be taking me into unknown pastures, and I don't want to miss anything along the way. I want a master who is clever enough, self confident enough, and controlled enough to manipulate the best out of me for both our pleasure.

I feel deliciously vulnerable under a master's power, and immensely little (a contradiction in terms, considering my size!), Maybe 'largely little' is better way of putting it, or even little in a big way, perhaps! Anyway, I want to offer myself up into it, except that I'm afraid to. I need to fold myself into my submission and wrap it around me until I am inside it, suckling and feeding on it. I'm not sure I like all the emotions, but I want to experience them all, just the same.

Vulnerability is like little prickly needles; seducing and painful and delicious! I'm apprehensive that I might get taken where I don't want to be, and left there and won't be able to get back. I'm excited because I want to be there. But I want to be brought back again, enhanced and stretched and having increased my carnal knowledge. Then I can work it into my own personal fabric, colour it in my own way, then feed it back again to the source of my erotic inspiration. I am, in fact, the world's most adventurous coward! As such, I am ripe for a master who isn't afraid of me and my fantastical needs, and can control me without fear; subtly and surely.

I would like to use this knowledge and awareness to paint sexually explicit pictures which challenge people to defy and deny that sexuality isn't omnipotent, and for all lesser men to know that they could satisfy their every whim, if they dared to take the plunge. I realise this is a very worrying line of thought as, again, it isn't very submissive at all!

I want my master to spank me. And, at the same time, I want to try and talk my way out of my spanking. I want to be punished like an errant child that's trying to push the limits and has reached the end of them. I want to know what's coming, so I can anticipate it, feel it, think it, breathe it.

I want my master naked and I want him dressed. I want him to touch me and maul me immediately upon meeting me. I want it to be known between us that he can take me whenever, wherever and however he chooses. A simple 'look' at any time can disarm me and throw me into sexual life. I'd then endure any sexual humiliation, because that's how I'd want it.

I want to feel the black leather glove entering and exploring. I'd have to adjust my stance to accommodate it so I could suckle it with my sex. But still, I'm not really sure of myself with men. I'm only just coming into my own with them. I love the smell of them, love the sense of them, but always confident, forceful men. I'm certainly not able to teach yet. I can only write about what I have experience of.

The master doesn't even need to be brutal with me. I don't need to be taught his strength, as I know it already. I need a sure hand, one who understands sexual pain to teach me to pleasure him and lift me through the pain barrier. He must be able to instinctively know when I'm ready to step up the 'gears', keep me riding the edge of climax or be able to pull me over in seconds. Teach me to suck cock better, deeper, longer than any woman has done it before.

I'm fascinated, totally fascinated, by the idea of having my body strapped up in different ways. I love it when my lover takes me to be fitted for a harness; made to stand while it's adjusted, tightened here, loosened there, fitted so my breasts are raised or dropped, pushed together or pulled apart.

Likewise, my buttocks are stretched wide, exposing my asshole, encouraging me to relax in readiness for my master to stretch it even wider in order to rape and plunder it. I'd like to be readied like a mare being fitted for a saddle. She's in use, but not quite beginning the build up yet, so she's fidgety. My master knows that she'll soon be of no use to him. All she wants is servicing. Studding her, mounting her, thrusting into her, biting her neck. Thrust long and hard into me/her, while she/me strains back to meet each thrust.

Maybe I'm a young filly, young and new, and this is my first heat and deep inside are animal urges I've never satisfied before. But I can't soften to them, can't accept them because the smell of the stallion excites me, so I buck and kick, thrash my head and stamp my feet. But he's ready, very ready. He's tries to mount me, but I run so he hobbles me, ties my feet apart and fastens my head. Even in his haste, he stops to smell me as I push out my wide open vagina, swollen and wet. He mounts in one swift, sure movement, thrusting his phallus straight in deep and begins thrusting, tight bucking. He shoots his load almost immediately. As he withdraws, a gush of spunk runs down over the backs of my thighs, hot and steaming.

I'd want my human lover to run his hand into it, massaging handfuls of it into my ass-hole, using it to lubricate his own way in. He would utilise my own recent use to his advantage, pushing me down at the shoulders, having my rear high, my hands behind my back, behind my neck, over my head, pushing as many fingers as he can into my hole, then fanning them out inside.

I'd want him to pretend this is the first time I've ever been spanked or handled roughly by a man. That first time he spanks me, I want him to spank me hard, I want it to be the spanking of my life, the first since I was a child. Done with passion, without restraint. Done until my tears flow freely and my vagina has opened, my bladder emptied, my ass-hole softened and he's stripped away the last of my inhibitions, reduced my body and taught my vagina a lesson it won't easily forget, open me to learn what comes next so that the thought of the spanking tightens me as you urge me to piss for you. I want my master to have that control of me, to be skilful enough to train my body functions to perform as he chooses.

Don't run, my master has commanded of me. Fickle bitch that I am, my tongue lolls in canine enthusiasm. Unlike a cat, I set no score by independence. Like a whore, I fawn at his feet, begging and whining to be dominated. He has use of me, touches me until I burn with desire. Works my sex until I climax, so I know he can do it; know he can bring me off as he chooses; know that, when he delays me, it is no accident. He makes me wait as long or as little as he desires; has me dancing to his tune.

God help me if we ever get 'thought police'. I am the least ordinary person leading the most ordinary life. People would cross themselves in horror if they could read my mind, know my daily thoughts. When I'm having an identity crisis (imagine if we all had an identity crisis at the same time!) I think I'm just an egotistical bitch and need a few lessons in humility. What a poor, unworthy thought? To think oneself like other people. To be ordinary.

I want to hear what my master thinks and wants. That's another reason why I think I'm submissive. I find it difficult to take the initiative, but I'm excellent when I'm told what to do. And that feeling is more pronounced with dominant people. I slip very easily into their shadow. I expect them to manipulate what they require from me. It's unlikely I'll take the lead, unless I'm taught to by my master. Maybe that's the difference between dominant and submissive. Dominants do, and submissives are done to. My master will know more about that than I do.

Chapter 6: Bronwyn

.

Age: 37, Former Nurse, living in Islington, London, UK

I have always been very submissive and, over the last ten years or so, I have been trying to find the perfect master, one who could totally control my mind and fulfil my needs as well as his own. My need was to feel owned and totally dominated. Over the years I've met many so-called masters through websites. Some of the replies were just nonstarters and, out of many, I picked out the few who sounded good only to be disappointed when we met. They were, inevitably, men simply looking for sex at the end of the day. I knew there had to be a 'real' master out there for me and, the more frustrated I got, the more I craved to meet the master I had fixed in my dreams.

By sheer luck I bought some old fetish magazines on eBay. These mags were all now out of print, but I loved reading them just the same. I read one article by a Master James of London called 'The Perfect Submissive'. An address was given to contact him. I felt it was a long shot that Master James would still be at that address, but I knew I just had to try it. My hand literally shook with nerves as I wrote a very respectful letter to him asking the master to forgive the impertinence of such an untrained submissive such as myself daring to be granted an interview. I posted off the letter and hoped that he would see fit to reply.

While waiting for his answer I read more articles in the magazines about Master James. There were also pictures of his slave, a very beautiful, dark haired girl in a leather body harness. She was so stunning that she made my heart sink to look at her. I thought Master James would never be interested in a late thirties woman like me when he could have his pick of all these younger girls.

You can imagine my joy when, a few days later, Master James actually replied to me! His letter was wonderfully simple and direct. It read: 'Ring me, bitch, on this number after 8pm'. He made no attempt to impress me like the others had done. His straightforward response let me know that it was I who must impress him! I rang him that evening as ordered. He told me straight away that he was not concerned about what age, size or shape a bitch was. What concerned him was that all his bitches should be 100% obedient. Not even 99% would do, they had to be the full 100% submissive before he would even consider granting them an interview. If that was me, he said, then he would consider my application.

I have to say that, even over the phone, I found Master James's voice to be full of confidence and dominance, but with understanding, as well, of my needs. I knew immediately that I just had to meet this wonderful sounding man! He told me later that what had surprised and pleased him about my letter was the way in which I had poured out my feelings to him. He said he had felt that I could be the perfect submissive for him, in the same way as I had felt him to be the perfect master for me! We talked at great length for over three hours and he arranged for me to come down to London from Wales, where I then lived, in two weeks time. I gave him my word I would be there as his last words to me were that he hated time wasters and warned me not to mess with him.

A date was given for me to come to him. I was to ring from the station upon arrival. I did as instructed and arrived at the station at the given time and called. He told me to catch a taxi to his address. As I walked to the taxi rank, however, I found myself gripped by a sudden, overwhelming fear. I had waited all these years to meet such a man; a master who was so genuine and so well known in the scene. Would I be good enough for him, would he send me away? The fear took control of my head and I ran back to the station and took the first train back home to Wales! As soon as the train moved off, however, I realised I was doing the wrong thing and throwing away perhaps the best opportunity I would ever have to give myself to a truly dominant man. I had simply blown it when I had come face to face with the real thing!

But it was too late now, I thought. Master James would never want me now. After letting almost a week go by, I wrote to him again begging his forgiveness and explaining the panic I had experienced and how much I regretted it now. To my delight Master James wrote back with a very understanding letter, but informing me that if this were to happen again there would be no more chances. Another date was set and this time I managed to control my fear and actually show up!

This time Master James told me to come to the tube station nearest his home and call him from there. He would come to pick me up. This time when I called, admittedly a little later than planned, his phone was engaged. I found out later that another dominant friend of his had rung up for a chat. Understandably, because I was a bit late in calling, he assumed I had lost my nerve again and had dismissed me as he had warned he would. After all, the master had two other slave girls at that time.

I waited at the tube station for an hour, trying his number every few minutes. But it remained engaged. Eventually, I decided to go around to his flat anyway. I mustered all my courage, knowing this was going to be a life changing night for me, and rang his intercom buzzer. A stern voice told me to come up to his flat. Opening the door, he told me to get in and take my coat off. I was delighted to see that Master James was pleased with what he saw as I was totally naked underneath.

I stammered out an apology for my lateness as I stood naked and trembling in his hallway. He was uninterested in my pathetic excuses and simply ordered me into his room where, he said, he would begin my training straight away. My first taste of real dominance came immediately when he informed me I was no longer to have a name. From hence forth, I was to be known simply as 'bitch' or 'it'. At last I was getting what I had only ever dreamed about!

Master and Bitch worked all weekend to bring me into shape and up to the sort of standards of obedience he expected from all his sluts. At night I slept on the floor beneath his bed. As only his Number Three Bitch at this time I was way down on the harem hierarchy and could not expect to be granted the privilege of sharing the master's bed at this early stage of my training. It didn't matter, it was enough for me to be allowed to serve. I was made even prouder when he informed me that he was very pleased with my progress that first weekend together, and that he felt I had the potential for total submission!

After that first weekend I returned home to Wales, but still rang my master every night. Yes, every night! Master James would continue my training during these phone sessions until I was totally dominated. Every time I called, master specified that I had to be naked and on my knees. To prove my nakedness to him, I was required to spank my own bottom so that he could hear it over the phone. He decided he would allow me to visit him every two weeks. That was seven months ago and, according to Master James, I have become a very highly trained and obedient bitch.

I am now completely shaved and I'm considered to be a very good fuck for anyone who Master James will let use me. What people outside this scene can't seem to understand is that this is a real situation. It's not a game. He owns me as his bitch. I am his property as much as that settee you're sitting on. I can never get my master out of my mind and I think about him all the time. I only want to serve him in any way he wishes. I feel lost without him and long always to be naked in his presence. I feel the happiest I have ever been in my life.

Master likes to let very vulgar-mouthed, older men use me. The more vulgar the better. He likes to start the proceedings with a bit of a show by having me exhibited in the cage with something like 'Fucking Slut' or 'Spank This Ass' written on my body. I'll then be made to walk around nude. Only no one is allowed to talk to me. They all just talk about me, or 'it', as Master James likes to refer to me. He likes them to act as if I'm not there, or I'm just a dumb animal at an auction. I love to listen to the filth they talk about me and discuss with each other what they intend doing with me.

Master James has certain limits to what he will let the men do. First, he will give me a sound thrashing in front of all these men. He will allow them to feel my tits, tie me up, pull my fanny open and have a good look and a grope. However, he doesn't like the men to spunk over me or slap my tits, which he considers to be a dangerous practice. He does allow other men to spank me, either bent over or in bondage. He also says I give a lovely hand job. They can stick bananas, cucumbers and candles up my fanny or the 'tradesmens'— as James call my rear passage! They can also eat straight out of my fanny, if they want to. He will allow men to finger fuck me, as well. I am trained now to masturbate two men together while sucking off a third man. A fourth can fuck me at the same time, as long as he agrees to wear a condom.

Of course, having me as his slave doesn't stop Master James from giving other women the chance to explore their fantasies with me. He is always looking for the best female submissives. They can be aged between eighteen and fifty, straight or bisexual, just so long as they are single and totally obedient. He is not interested in looks or body shape. Though he does rather like women with big bottoms that he can use as a pillow. Although my master makes sure his other slaves are not around when I visit, I am used to the idea of sharing him with other submissive women.

Though I realise I am not the only slave-slut in his life, I am still deeply honoured to be able to call myself one of Master James' bitches. I know he will only accept true submissive women and will turn down, what he considers to be 'play actors', so I am in the very best of company. He is understanding enough to keep most of his bitches separate and trains them on different nights, so they never meet. However, I know some who are bisexual are allowed to play together to amuse him. As I am bisexual myself, I don't mind how many other females there are, but to date I haven't been trained with any of them.

In the future, Master James is considering allowing me to move in as a full time slave. He wants to have me tattooed and pierced to his specifications. He also wants to take me to London fetish clubs and have me used by groups of men, up to twenty at a time. I only live now to serve my master, and will comply with all of his demands without question.

Chapter 7: Lucy

Age: 29, Waitress, living in Boston, USA

Before meeting my current boyfriend I had, had several sexual relationships, of which none provided me with real sexual gratification. Oh, I enjoyed the sex, but there was no 'big bang', if you know what I mean. Then I met Rick, and my sex life changed (boy, did it ever change!), drastically.

At first I thought Rick was quite overbearing. Whatever we did, wherever we went, was always what he wanted to do. I was never asked what I wanted to do, or where I wanted to go, but somehow I found myself actually enjoying being told what we were going to do, where we were going to do it, and what time I was to be ready. And sometimes he even dictated what I was to wear, and the more we dated, the more I came to expect it.

My first S&M experience came shortly after I had fallen head over heels in love with Rick. At that point in our relationship I would have walked through fire for him. Whatever Rick told me to do, I would do just to please him. And then came my first big shock and what would lead me into my present submissive relationship with him.

The two of us were in our favourite drinking bar with a couple of his male friends when he leaned over and whispered in my ear that one of them, a guy I didn't find attractive called Larry, wanted to fuck me and that it would be alright with him if I would do it. My first reaction was total shock. Just the thought of being with a man

I had no feelings for was quite repulsive to me. I told Rick that I just couldn't do such a thing and that I was surprised, to say the least, that he had even dared ask me. Then he dropped a real bomb-shell on me. He said straight out that I would do it or I could move out and our relationship would be finished.

At that point I got up from the table, angry as hell, and informed him that I would be moving out right away. I literally ran out of the bar in tears and was soon back in Rick's house still crying my eyes out as I packed my suitcases. Halfway through packing my second suitcase I stopped, lay down on the bed and began thinking about what Rick had asked me to do. I also thought about the feelings I had for him, and at that moment I knew I didn't want to live without him, I trusted him, in spite of what he'd asked of me, and suddenly felt overwhelmed by the thought of being totally submissive to him in every way. My mind just flipped over, I guess.

I sat there on the bed, still weeping, hoping Rick would forgive me for embarrassing him in front of his friends. I found myself actually blaming myself for his anger at me. For over an hour I waited there thinking about the situation. After all, I reasoned to myself, it was such a simple thing he'd asked me to do. It would have been a quick fuck, and then it would have been over with. All I had to do was lie there and spread my legs.

When he finally came through the door I literally ran to him, threw my arms around him, and begged for his forgiveness. I told him that if he let me stay I would let Larry, or any friend of his, fuck me anytime they wanted to. You will never know how relieved I was when my apology was accepted. So that was the way the whole 'sub' thing started for me.

Rick informed me that from now on, if I wanted to be his live-in girlfriend, I must do exactly as I was told. For disobeying him earlier I was to be tied face down on the bed and have my back and bottom thoroughly thrashed with his belt. Of course, I was shocked at this sudden turn of events as well as the cruelty in his voice that I'd never heard before. I had figured he would have simply called his friend up, tell him to get over and fuck me, and that would be it. Now, you might have thought that I would have refused this new demand, but no, I simply accepted this, something had 'clicked' inside me.

Rick ordered me to strip naked on the spot, lay down on my stomach on the bed, and get myself into position to be spread-eagled. I did it without a second thought and was soon tightly bound, completely at his mercy. I now expected to feel the bite of his belt slamming down against my back and buttocks, but this was not what he had in mind. Not yet anyway. Rick left the bedroom, closed the door behind him, leaving me to lie there in solitude for almost an hour. When the door reopened, I could see Rick was not alone. Behind him was the friend I was supposed to fuck. Larry pulled a chair up in front of the bed and, because of the way my legs were so widely spread, I knew he had a really intimate view!

It was at this point I felt this stirring in my pussy, and the wetness that quickly followed. Later I was to find that it wasn't just being looked at that turned me on, but the feeling of complete helplessness and the knowledge that my body was at the mercy of someone else who was about to beat me. And, all the while this was happening, there would be someone watching me, seeing me totally naked, someone other than my boyfriend and that was really turning me on!

Rick now blindfolded me. He didn't want me to see when the belt was being raised. This way he knew I couldn't anticipate the blow, only feel its sting when it came cracking down on my naked flesh. My body stiffened as I waited for the first blow and, when it came, just across the shoulder blades, it felt like my entire back had been soaked in flame. I cried out in excruciating pain as my body jerked. The second cut came down directly across the centre of my buttocks. Again I screamed, my body jerking wildly in reaction to the stinging blow.

Lash after lash crisscrossed my back and buttocks. One scream followed another as pain surged through me. I have no idea how many times he hit me, but between the blows I was fully aware of Larry's presence witnessing my welt-covered body and wet pussy.

And, believe it or not, I actually had an orgasm while Rick was lashing me. And, needless to say, when that first climax ripped through my body, I was taken completely by surprise.

Finally, my punishment came to an abrupt end. I was untied from the bed, the blindfold removed, and ordered to give Larry a blowjob. Obediently, I dropped to my knees in front of him, my eyes staring at the hard bulge pressing against his fly, knowing it would soon be in my mouth. I crawled up between his legs, unzipped his fly and gently removed his hard-on. Once again I was surprised at the sudden desire I felt rushing through my pussy. I took Larry's hard cock in my hand and began licking the cock-end in earnest while Rick watched. Moments later I was practically swallowing the whole damn thing down my throat without needing to be told!

While I was sucking on Larry's prick, Rick began shooting the action on his phone camera—close-ups of my lips locked tightly around his friends' cock and my nose pressed hard into his hairy crotch seemed to be his favourite bits, as I recall. After watching this for a while, Rick decided it was time for the fucking I'd run away from in the bar. He told Larry to get me up on the bed on my knees and spread my legs far apart. He followed quickly behind me. I felt his hard cock-end searching for the entrance to my soaking pussy and, when he found it, slowly eased himself into me.

I let out a long satisfying sigh. The feelings of total uncomplicated lust, feelings I'd never experienced before were rampaging though my entire being at this point. Every nerve ending was extremely sensitive to his slightest touch. And, to top it off, I actually got a thrill out of being recorded and watched by my boyfriend while I was doing it. This was something I could never have imagined myself doing, even a few short hours earlier.

It was only a matter of seconds before I had another orgasm as Larry came as well. I could hear him moan above me as he unloaded himself into me. When Larry pulled out, Rick got up on the bed in front. His prick was sticking up like a flag pole and, knowing what he wanted, I slipped my lips around it and began sucking on it like it was a lollipop. He was so incredibly horny after watching his friend fuck me that, only moments after shoving his cock into my mouth, I could feel it throbbing against my tongue and I knew he was coming. Sure enough, a second later and his cock was out of my mouth and he shot his cum all over my face.

Both men now stood beside the bed looking down at me. Cum was running down my cheeks, burning my right eye, a glob of it even stuck up my nose. It oozed out of my pussy and down the insides of my thighs. I knew I probably looked a mess, but at that point I really didn't care. For some unknown reason I knew that this would be the beginning of a new life style for me, and that Rick would be my master for as long as he wanted to be. I knew right then that I would be incapable of doing anything other than what he wanted me to do.

The next day, after my ordeal with the belt and Larry fucking me, I found out that I was to be punished further. First my pussy was shaved completely bald and I was given orders to keep it that way. After I shaved my pussy, I spread my legs wide for his approval. I was then given a very tight fitting sweater to put on. The sweater had two neatly trimmed holes through which each of my breasts were to poke through. When I bent over my skirt slid up completely exposing my ass cheeks. I was handed a pair of red heels and told to put them on. The heels were a good five inches high, and at first I found it really difficult standing in them, let alone walking.

Next came my punishment. Rick wet his fingers and made my nipples harden up by pinching and pulling on them. He then produced two metal clamps with gold chain hanging from them. These clamps are called 'alligator' clamps. Each clamp has tiny, sharp teeth along each side, and at the end of each chain there is a small hook. My body stiffened in anticipation of the pain which I knew was about to come. Focusing on my right nipple to begin with, Rick opened one of the ugly, little things and fixed it in place. When the jaws closed down I could see and feel the teeth biting into my flesh. I really let out a loud cry of pain, begging Rick to take it off. But Rick wasn't about to change his mind.

A moment later I cried out again and, once more, my cry was met with another rebuttal. Two weights were then hung at the end of each chain which pulled my nipples and breasts sharply downward sending pain ripping straight through the centres of each breast and into my chest. Rick then told me I was to do all of today's chores with the weights suspended from my nipples. He said if he saw me without the clamps fixed at any time of the day, he would simply put them back and the punishment would last twice as long.

And that wasn't all. Next he had me bend over, spread my legs, and hold my ass-cheeks apart. He greased my ass real good, and then I felt something pressing up against the hole. I realised later that it was a butt plug. Thankfully, one of the smaller models. I still begged him not to do it, as this strange new thing invading me was pretty scary for me. But I guess you can imagine how that went. I got slapped across my ass for my trouble, followed by a real pain in the butt as he slammed the fucking thing straight into me. According to Rick's way of reckoning things, it was time to start stretching me out down there, for future fucking sessions.

As I did the chores, the weights swung back and forth, pulling on my nipples. At the same time the butt plug wiggled back and forth adding to my pain. Most surprising of all though, my pussy stayed wet the entire time, and by noon all I could think about was getting fucked. I didn't even care who fucked me, just so long as I had somebody's cock giving me what I needed. What a complete slut I'd become!

It was around one o'clock in the afternoon when the doorbell rang, and Rick told me to see who it was. Of course I told him I couldn't possibly go to the door with my tits sticking out of my sweater, weights hanging down from my nipples and a plug sticking out from my ass, but, as usual, my whining didn't get me anywhere and I had to go as I was anyway.

I opened the door to find Larry and another friend of Rick's who I didn't know. I later found out his name was George and that he was as cruel and dirty as Larry and Rick. Naturally, being men, their eyes went immediately to my tits. Without hesitation, Larry, who seemed to think I was common property after having me already, reached out, grabbed one of the weights, and gave it a sharp tug. I positively yelped as my tit was stretched forward, adding to the pain it was already in. But these two guys just laughed, keeping their eyes glued to my stretched breast. Larry pulled as hard on the weight as the chain would allow, then released it, letting it fall straight down. The following sharp pain to my nipple was almost unbearable.

I stood back from the door, allowing the two men to enter. They sat down in the living room, their eyes constantly glancing up at me and, above their chatter about sex and S&M, Rick ordered me to get them each a beer. When I turned my back to them it was their laughter that really got to me. I knew they could see the butt plug sticking out of my ass and felt a flush of shame and embarrassment rush over me as their laughter grew louder and cruder.

Returning from the kitchen, I handed each man a bottle. Rick angrily informed me I would have to be punished for being, as he crudely put it, so 'fucking dumb' in not thinking to bring his guests some beer without needing to be told. First, I was ordered to turn around, bend over, raise my skirt, spread my legs, and let them all get a good look at my pussy and at the butt plug sticking out of my ass-hole. Now the embarrassment and shame at having to expose myself with the plug protruding seemed a thousand times worse. I had to force myself to turn with my back to all three men and, as I bent forward, I could feel the hem of my skirt raise up over my naked buttocks. I spread my legs as far apart as I could, struggling to stay on the five inch heels!

I was then ordered to run my fingertip around my ass-hole. With feelings of more shame and embarrassment, I did it. Not content with this humiliation, Rick then demanded that I removed the butt plug with my finger. I immediately grabbed the shaft of the plug to do his bidding. Even though the thing was mercifully small, it still produced a considerable amount of pain as it spread the muscles around my ass-hole wider and wider before finally popping out.

Now, with the butt plug removed, I was to told to push my finger into the hole and finger fuck myself. I heard lewd chuckles and derisive comments from the men gathered behind me, but at this point I didn't care how much I was humiliating myself, all I wanted was the feelings of orgasm rushing through my body.

After watching me finger fucking my ass hole for a couple of minutes, Rick ordered me to give me them all a blow-job. I slowly turned round to face them, and found three hard cocks jutting straight out at me from their open flies. Kneeling down between George's parted legs, I took his thick cock into my mouth and began sucking. Rick told me I was not to spend more than three minutes with each cock before switching to the next. He timed my actions on his watch and ordered the changes. In all I must have spent fifteen minutes at it because I know I did each man five times over with some pretty vigorous sucking!

Then I was ordered to lie on my back on the coffee table and spread my legs again. Each man then took it in turns to slam their cocks in and out of my pussy, during which time I had four intense orgasms. They all managed to hold back on their own for what would be the final glory. When it came time, Rick told them to stand over my face and continue jacking off till they all shot, almost simultaneously, over me.

After they had gone, I was given orders not to wash my 'whores face', as Rick called it, for the rest of the day. I was to let their cum dry, hard and crusty, and every time Rick would look at me and laugh that lewd laugh of his. It made me feel even more like a whore. Of course this also turned me on, and at the end of the day, when I was finally allowed to shower up and clean up, I was totally ready for another good fucking.

Rick took me into the bedroom, made me lay across his naked lap so I could feel his hard prick pressing up against my pussy mound, and paddled me until I was literally begging him to take me like the wanton slut I'd become. My ass was red and very sore when he pushed me from his lap, landing me, with a yelp, on the floor on my aching bottom. He just picked me up like a discarded rag doll, threw me down on the bed, pushed my legs wide apart, and fucked me silly.

Today, after many, many masochistic experiences, I wouldn't dream of having sex without being severely punished or sexually humiliated in some way first, it becomes completely addictive. The punishment to my tits, nipples, pussy, or whatever brings me a kind of climax I'd never imagined possible before. Do I feel sexually used? Not on your life, no way! I wouldn't change my present lifestyle. You could say Rick forced me, but he just awakened a tendency I already had—without fully understanding it, and I made the choice to give him that complete control. I love the pain, love the humiliation, and the sexual degradation. Some will make judgments, I know, but the excitement it gives me, I can't get any other way now, pretty fucking weird for some folks I know, but that's just the way it is for me.

When Rick has men over for an evening of using me, I think I look forward to it as much, if not more so than he does. I wouldn't have imagined myself saying this before that first night in the bar with Rick and his friend when I ran out crying like a silly school girl, but there's just something about being tortured and fucked by strangers that is a real turn on for me. I suppose you could say I've really got in touch with my 'inner-slut'— fuck the 'goddess'!

Chapter 8: Patty

Age: 32 , Handmaiden to Ms Christine Deering of the Femina Society, Location: Maryland, USA

During the past seven and a half years of my servitude to Ms Christine. I have understood what it is like to be really cared for and trained by a Dominant woman who really believes in me. She has shown me how to be proud of myself and my accomplishments. She has helped me mature in ways I had never thought possible. Ms C. has taken the time and patience to make me the kind of slave she is proud to own. I am very proud to belong to her. I serve her out of love and adoration. Our lifestyle is quite real for us. It is not just a 'kinky' game, nor is it just sexual fantasy. I am her slave first, her significant other second, as well as her friend and her companion. We share a very unique relationship that others who only play at S&M could never even begin to understand. There is nothing wrong with a persons fantasies in this lifestyle even if they are only acted out in the bedroom. However, Mistress and I both wanted and searched for something more serious than just a fantasy.

Maybe I should hold up for a minute here and explain what the Femina Society is about for the benefit of those who don't know. The Society is an organisation, based here in the United States, and its avowed aim is to promote female supremacy in a matriarchal society. It is very spiritual in its leanings toward all the feminine archetypes found in such belief systems as Paganism and Hinduism. A person may be a male or a female who wants to surrender to feminine authority in all aspects of their life as a submissive. All men are expected to be submissive. A woman may work toward the rule of women either as a Dominant, like my Mistress, or as a handmaiden who serves other women, such as myself. But it must be made absolutely clear that no woman in the Society ever serves a man in anyway, shape or form! In our world the male will find a life of useful servitude as his ever-lasting reward, while the woman will discover a Sisterhood that offers both a shared vision and practical support for her chosen lifestyle.

The would-be slave, whether male or female, must go through a pretty tough training process before being admitted into the Society. During this initial period they will learn the moist basic tenant of the Society; namely, that a slave is not free and has no free time. Free time is for free people! All my time belongs to my instructress/owner and, through her, the Femina Society as a whole.

The first part of my training to serve Ms C consisted of what we call 'sensual servitude' including massage, body worship and serving Mistress as her toilet when she needed to go to the bathroom. A further aspect of my training was the serious study of Female Supremacy. Why it's natural, why it's right and why it's necessary in the world today more than ever before. I had to study serious books on the natural superiority of women, the origins of human society as a matriarchy and how the patriarchy has unnaturally reversed the roles of the sexes and oppresses women. Next come lessons in honesty, loyalty and how to be a proper and pleasing servant. This means learning to do useful work and live only to please the Mistress, effacing one's own wants and desires. The would-be slave is also trained in networking to promote the growth of the Society and spread it's goals.

The Femina Society consists of a Mother Chapter, Sister Chapters and Associate Branches. The Mother Chapter is located in New England and organises all aspects of the Society's work. Education is carried out through the School For Servants and the Centre For Matriarchal Studies. Networking is carried out by communication with Sister Chapters, Associate Branches, and other non-member

Dominas, mailing projects and advertising. The Mother Chapter is the final authority in all matters concerning the Society, especially membership, but works closely with Sister Chapters. These Chapters are established under the auspices of a Chapter Leader; that is, a Domina who wishes to promote the teachings and goals of The Femina Society in her geographical area.

Anyway getting back to what I was saying earlier about my own personal feelings. The only thing that bothers me these days is some of the lack of respect towards Dominants that I have heard about and witnessed. A Dominant deserves to be treated with respect such as addressing them by their title, and always kneeling or sitting on the floor in their presence. If a submissive is owned by a Dominant or even just serving one temporarily, they should always remember to ask permission before they smoke cigarettes in front of them or drink alcohol in their presence. I personally do not know of any true Dominant who will tolerate a drunken, out of control submissive or one who is high on any kind of drug. It is not a safe way to play if one is under the influence of any substance.

I take my role very seriously. In the past, if a submissive would be disrespectful or disobedient towards a Dominant, that would earn them a serious punishment or maybe even dismissal, never to serve that Dominant again. I know that these beliefs still exist, but I have also heard about so-called submissives who are continually getting away with these infractions. This is very sad to me. If one calls oneself a submissive, then they should at least give that Dominant all their respect and obedience. All subs make mistakes now and then.

I am glad that things are different now and that submissives are treated like real people who have feelings and needs. I am very happy about the safety issues that are now being practised between Dominants and submissives. However, we as submissives should also understand that the

Word submission means just that; to "submit", to give another control. Respect is not a word that should just be used at the moment one is getting one's needs fulfilled by a Dominant.

I know that there are those who would never understand my

feelings because S&M is just a sexual fantasy to them. However, if you are truly a submissive who believes the way I do, always remember that the Dominant you are serving and submitting to will see and feel that real submission. True submission is very rare and a very special gift that we as submissives give to our Dominants. A true Dominant will expect you to understand that the time they spend training and playing with you should always be appreciated.

When I give of myself to my Owner or a Dominant Female that she may allow to play with me now and then in her presence, I do so to make Ms C proud of me. It makes me very happy to show others my submission. I trust my Owner with my life and I trust her judgement in who she allows to dominate me. I will endure as much as I possibly can for her or anyone of her choice. I am very proud of who I belong to and who I have become because of her.

When others refer to me as a 'legend' or the 'infamous' submissive, it makes me blush. I see myself as an experienced submissive who has learned a lot over the years of my servitude to Dominants and has grown into a person who is much more secure and happy than I have ever been in my life. I have made mistakes along the way and have suffered emotional hurt and upheaval. But I proved myself stronger than I realised because I didn't allow past events to discourage me from my search to find what I wanted and needed from the right live-in situation.

I am a submissive who loves with my heart, submits with my inner soul and being, and tries my best to please my Owner and make her proud to call me her property. In the past ten years before I met Ms C., I had 'danced on the edge' but now I have found a stable and caring environment within our chosen lifestyle.

Chapter 9: Anne

Age: 56, Civil Servant, living in Kent, UK.

Last week I went to meet my new Master. He had not dealt with me before, but we had met. We enjoyed a meal and a few glasses of wine in a rather nice restaurant. He is handsome and I admit much too young for me! Yet he seems somehow to have that firmness a Master needs. And from the first he was somehow in charge. I liked that feeling.

I was not sure that a man of younger years would want me. I am all too aware that a man of thirty could be my son! Oh, such wicked thoughts run through my mind at the thought of it! For which I shall no doubt deserve the discipline he may decide to give me. May I say that I am definitely not one of those who profess to be a slave yet insist on a 'code' word to use when the master is going beyond their limits. How can one be a slave and wish to set limits in such a way? I may cry and beg and grovel, but I still accept my Masters wishes over my own.

Anyway, I had worn my charcoal suit and a blue silk blouse. My mid-heeled and dark stockings. I wore only a touch of lipstick as I wanted to be 'respectable' as far as the world was concerned, at least! During the year my Master made it clear that he would use me as he saw fit. I would be given the severest discipline and I would be made to suffer. My obedience would be an instant and automatic response. He did not, thankfully, seem disappointed in my appearance. Yet he did not compliment me on my clothes or my manner.

However I seem to pass his scrutiny. I was given my orders and he wrote his number where I was to ring and confirm my acceptance of his authority.

Then in a gentlemanly way he walked me back to my car. Once there he ordered me (my first test of obedience) to kneel on the wet and muddy ground, half hidden by the door of his car. I obeyed at once. Later, at home, I found that my stockings and shoes were all scuffed and ruined- but I didn't care.

My Master (for at that moment there was no doubt he was my Master) said not a word. But, as I grovelled on the wet and muddy ground, he slapped me so hard across the face that I felt my lips sore against my teeth. Looking up, with my face raised to this lovely man who stood over me, I realised in the half dark of the car park he had undone himself and had pulled out his lovely cock for me to honour with my mouth.

I knew my duty.

Even as my sore lips opened and I learned my head forward to perform my sacred task. I knew my that Master was testing my sincerity in wanting to be his and to be used as he wished. I love to do that to a man. It is so lovely an act of homage, well, it is to me. I won't (can't) describe my long and loving fellatio of my now true Master, or my pleasure as he gave me his own pleasure in my mouth. In this way I show my love or, in 'our' world, my submission.

When I had done my duty and had used my tongue to make sure his cock was completely clean, I was allowed to stand up. I stood there, my lips split, but I didn't care. My skirt was all wet and dirty around the hem, but it didn't matter.

No kisses. No words.

He told me when to ring and then was gone. Yet, oh God, I knew I had passed his test; that I was his to use, to whip and to hurt for as long as it amused him.

So now I am getting ready for him again.

I bathe and powder my body. I even admire myself and consider that my old body is not that bad. I must be as nice as I can, even though my bottom and thighs will, I know, be in a few hours red and wealed, or worse, from my Master's blows. A 'shameless old cow' my Master said I was, and it's true! I wonder if he would not want a more fuller bosomed woman. Though my nipples are compensated for by my 'rings'. I have one in each breast, above the teat, and a big one in my mound. Will he like them? I use cream to rub into the holes. After a bath they are dry and feel tight. I use my red rouge, too, around each teat and a trace on my cunt. When he sees and feels my overused and overdeveloped sex will he be disgusted at me? Too late now. In two hours he will have me before him. I decide to wear my pale beige camisole. As I dress I begin to feel so afraid of what is in store for me. It is a strange, wonderful feeling.

My Master has ordered me to wear a short skirt and dark stockings, my usual elastic topped ones. He must know that my fat knees and thighs look vulgar in a short thing. But he ordered me to get one, so I have. I wear a little lipstick and brush a little matt on my face. I don't look too bad, I think. At least he won't be ashamed of me, anyway. But my fat bum and flabby thighs in that short skirt! Does he intend to make me look vulgar, like a whore? At last I leave. I put on my long camel coat with the big sleeves and again, as ordered, high heels. These I find so awkward, but I want to wear them, so I have no choice.

I drive to the place he ordered and leave my car. Not much is said when we meet." You came then? You know I'm going to thrash you?" I answer, half scared, no fully terrified! "Yes, Master." Then we go by cab to his place. On the way, he tells the driver to stop in a street where a lot of prostitutes gather. He orders me to go into a shop and buy condoms. Oh, the exquisite shame of it all! My red face, my wet feeling!

At last to his house.

We go in. He takes my coat. Not much is said. I am ordered to turn around and display myself for my Master's inspection. He tells me I am an old whore and that he hates whores, so will punish me. He makes me kneel on the rug in his sitting room. He has a whisky. He does not offer me one. I kneel in loving dread of him. What will he do with me? Wild, mad thoughts run through my head and make me even wetter.

Still kneeling I move slightly in order to get more comfortable and earn a hard slap on the face. He orders me to keep still while he leaves the room for a moment. Naturally, I do as I am told. He returns with a long, thin cane. He orders me to remove my blouse. I obey with trembling fingers. He draws the straps of my bra down. I am now completely bare to the waist. I feel so exposed to him. He feels my shoulders and my back like I am an animal at an auction. I feel his fingers trace one of my old scars that was given to me by my husband so long ago. Lastly, he runs his hands around to feel my bosom. Christ, I scream silently, he's pulling on my tit-rings! He pulls so hard it is all I can do to stop from crying out. He pulls even harder, dragging me forward so that I am bent to the ground. Then he pulls me up again. Now I am sobbing uncontrollably. My tits hurt terribly. Disregarding my pain, he orders me to put my hands behind my head and not to move. Then, with a tone of contempt in his voice, he tells me my tits are hardly worth caning, they are so small. But perhaps they are tender, he adds cruelly. "Let's find out, shall we?" he says and brings the cane down hard on my poor tender breasts. I try not to scream, but fail. It hurts so I can't not let out the pain. It is too much for me to stay silent. He is marking me terribly. Each swish of the cane leaves a thin red line. He doesn't care how hard he hits or where. On my nipples it seems to cut me; on my rings it makes a click sound.

My Master pushes me forward so that my head touches the rug and he proceeds to cane my exposed thighs. This makes me cry even more till I topple over onto the floor. At last he rests and sits, calmly watching me as I lie sobbing. Then he says it is time for me to be really whipped!

I am ordered to stand and strip off completely. He is critical of me and calls me a fat-assed old whore. I am told to bend over the back of a large couch. My head hangs now. My legs sting from the bite of the cane and my tits are on fire. And now he is bringing the crop! Doesn't he know a man can destroy a woman so easily with a crop? He knows but does not care. Is this to be my fate? It is not for me to say. It is only my place to obey. And I will even if it does destroy me.

Chapter 10: Imogen

Age: 41, Financial Director, living in East Dulwich, London, UK

Frustration was the key reason I slid into playing the submissive. Sexual frustration was the driving force behind turning that want and need into a real living experience. But how does one find the intro? How does one find the right kind of partner, or partners? Less difficult if you're male. There are numerous girls you can visit to experience an hour or so of slavery, bondage, humiliation and servitude. Almost impossible if you're female. My first real kick was as a teenager seeing the film, 'Nine and half weeks', which was slammed by the some for portraying females as being submissive to violent and controlling men. I'd read the damning articles and, as a result, became even more eager to see the movie!

My boyfriend at the time, who was incapable of ever displaying dominant tendencies, had the dubious pleasure of escorting me to see the film. Actually, it was his idea, strangely enough! Anyway, I found myself sitting in the cinema, mouth wide open and with an aching, desperate need inside I knew only too well as a deep, strong sexual urge. The urge would not abate and, as I've already explained, my boyfriend was not the one to fulfil it. He was dumped very soon after this, unsurprisingly enough.

This was best for both of us, in retrospect. I now recognised that, while being submissive or masochistic does not make you cruel and heartless (we leave that to the dominants and sadists!), it does make you more demanding and exacting of your partners. Ironically, a submissive woman will only let herself be dominated by someone she deems worthy of the prize. Suddenly, when sizing up a suitable partner, your 'shopping list' of qualities that you'd look for alters completely. Looks, sensible job, associated good stable income take second place to natural dominance and the ability to wield a whip! Can he get turned on by putting me into bondage or spanking me? Ultimately, is he sexually adventurous? Once all those answers are ticked, then a relationship can commence.

Women become submissive or desire playing the submissive role in their sex lives for a wide range of reasons. Sexual psychotherapists argue that the desire to be dominated stems from feelings of self worth, or a history of child sexual abuse, or low self confidence. This may be so in some cases, I cannot comment. I can only say that, as a professional, university educated, middle class woman who is highly successful in her career, I certainly don't feel I fit into the pigeon hole of typically abused, no-hoper!

In fact, it was very probably my own success that created that need to be controlled after work. Taking the lead in the office, ordering people around and having so much responsibility and, I suppose, power, sparked off this desire to hand over the reigns to someone else in my private life. Really, I felt no different from those executives who go to visit a dominatrix. Except that I was a woman and needed that kind of ritualised abuse from a man which, I've come to understand, raises a whole hornets nest of feminist arguments.

In those first few months, after ditching the boyfriend, I went through a strange variety of men. Usually older, not exactly handsome, and sometimes downright unpleasant. They all had to be tried and tested in my desperate search for that elusive 'dominant' character. The trouble was that the more submissive I became (and by submissive, I mean sexually submissive only, I am definitely not submissive in any other aspect of my life), the more demanding of my lovers I became.

My fantasies became, correspondingly, more severe and extreme. I remember one potential lover literally gave up the struggle.

He ended up, poor soul, with his head in his hands, sitting on the edge of my bed, almost sobbing as he admitted he couldn't hurt me. I tried to explain that I didn't want him to permanently hurt me. I just wanted him to make me scream and beg for forgiveness. It was no good. My requests left him completely mystified. Another lover dumped! From then on, and for the next few months I would go out of my way to find the kind of men I would never meet in my ordinary, well-ordered, middle class life. I picked up men through contact mags in rough pubs, even on the street. Anyone who seemed dominant or came across like a brute would be enough to fire my lust and my hopes.

After a succession of very short-lived relationships (if they can even be called that!), Which I can only describe as empty and totally unsatisfactory, I found myself close to despair. The problem was that, the more dissatisfied I became after each attempt to find love and servitude in one lover, the higher and more insanely unrealistic my expectations became. I knew I was spiralling out of control, hooked on my ideal notion of the perfect submissive 'fuck' with, it seemed to me, ever diminishing chances of realising it.

Yes, sex was very much part of the equation for me. I know many people in the fetish scene feel that the full sex act has no place in the art of domination, but I disagreed. I wanted to be tied to the bed and made accessible from all directions and angles. I needed to be forced to suck cock and to beg for more. I wanted to act the complete slut (which, of course, I never was or, at least, would never admit to being). I fantasised about being tortured, spanked and whipped. All these thoughts went through my mind endlessly. And the more I failed to realise them, the more intense they would become.

I started buying literature and props and bondage equipment for myself. I would put myself in bondage, even whip myself to get the high I craved. I kept all my paraphernalia tucked away in the wardrobe, as guilty as anyone else who has a terrible secret. That's the way I felt, anyway. I would masturbate myself every night, listening to the voice of my imaginary, idealised, lover in my head, as he ordered me to do it this way and that; in front of mirrors, in front of his friends, even live on stage at some seedy sex club. In my imagination, he would take me to expensive restaurants where I would be dressed very provocatively. At the end of the meal I would be forced to lay down on the table and be used by all the waiters as a means of paying the bill.

My imagination knew no boundaries. Sometimes I was a servant girl abused by the master of the house, other times I was a sex slave to a cruel horse trader in the desert, or a curious and rare white slave to a big black prince in some unknown African state. My genitals and nipples would be pierced and adorned with elaborate and exquisite jewels. Condoms and any notion of 'safe sex' were dismissed by my primitive masters, as chief after chief took me at his will. My body knew no limits as I was subjected to repeated beatings and punishments; each becoming increasingly more painful and arduous. Though I enjoyed all these scenarios in my imagination, I had still had sense enough to leave them there.

Being 'forced' to do all these things somehow removed the guilt. I was always helpless to protest in these situations and, indeed, when I did on occasion meet someone suitable in real life with whom to enact these fantasies, the subsequent orgasm would come more easily and more powerfully, gaining more mental release, the tighter the restraints of the mental bonds became. Free from guilt and safe in my ropes.

Real life experiences were, of course, played out with code words and within the bounds of safety and sanity! I dabbled with the fetish club scene for a while, and met some so-called 'masters' at parties and events. While many were very pleasant men, I found the whole thing ultimately a bit disappointing. I came to the conclusion that most were no more than fantasists themselves who were really quite weak in their own lives, and whose dominant natures went about as deep as their leather costumes. Either that, or they were quite horrible men who had some sort of chip on their shoulders, and were obvious women haters who just wanted to get their own back against the female sex for whatever reason, by beating the hell out of a girl. And I'm not that much of a masochist! As I said earlier they really have to deserve the prize and frankly they didn't.

I think the fetish scene works best on the Fem-Dom side which, unfortunately, is not where I'm coming from. I think the women look great and it's wonderful that they, and their subs, can express themselves through such creative role-play. But, at the end of the day, I was seeking something a lot more than dressing up and play acting. In the end, I gave up on the fetish scene altogether, as far as my own needs went. As I am quite an assertive person in my own right, I have my own home and career and all the rest of it, I'm very independent. A real product of Mrs Thatcher's generation of go-for-it women, I suppose. I certainly don't need a man in my life as husband and provider. I can do all that perfectly well myself, thank you very much. What I needed was someone who could put me under their thumb in a purely sexual sense.

The closest I've come to my ideal (who is also my current playmate) is someone I would never have dreamed of meeting if I'd not undertaken this adventure in my life. For a start, he's black and lives a life-style that is, quite frankly, on a different planet to my own world of dealing with big blue-chip clients in a marketing company. But then, that's what I wanted.

I met Tyson at a club in South London where I'd gone with one date. This particular guy had a big thing about seeing me with other men, which was the reason he'd taken me to this club. His sexual fantasies invariably revolved around scenarios of me with big black 'monster' cocks, you know that whole 'cuckold' thing. Secretly, I think he was a bit 'bi' and actually wanted to be the one being fucked by a black cock. We never got that far in our relationship to find out, because the first club he took me to his fantasies came true, unfortunately without him along to enjoy the view!

I must admit I'd fantasised about black men, but had never had the opportunity to meet any socially in the circles I moved. I found it fascinating. The club was purely black. Though there were a lot of white women females in the club, there were no white guys, apart from this guy who'd brought me. Though I had already written off my date as unsuitable material for my needs, I suppose it was quite brave of him to venture into this place at all.

It wasn't long at all before I got approached for a dance by one of the black guys. What impressed me was how bold they all were in asking, as if a refusal had never crossed their minds. I have to say I found this quite new and, yes, exciting. Later, I understood the reason for their confidence. All of the white women who came to the club were interested only in black lovers. The women were, for the most part, thirty and forty some things, middle class, career women like myself. Teachers, social workers, feminists. The kind of modern, independent, politically correct women who would have been outraged if a white man displayed the sort of chauvinist behaviour I saw going on all around me. Yet, these same women not only tolerated it, they positively lapped it up from a black man! It was an eye-opener to a whole new world that I never knew existed, and I was fascinated.

Before the evening was over the date I'd arrived with had been rudely dismissed and I was with my new black lover. The danger of that first night will stay with me forever. Tyson's world was one of drugs and prostitutes and gangsters. I was completely out of my depth, but loved every minute of it. As long as I knew that, at the end of the experience, I could retreat to my safe, middle class cosiness. Most exciting of all was that I knew I was going to be fucked that night; that my opinion on the matter was almost inconsequential. In fact, that first time, he didn't even wait to take me home to bed, but fucked me in the men's toilets at the club. Once back at his he revealed his 'kinkier' side. Without hardly a word he tied me up on his bed on my front and thrashed me with a tawse, before blindfolding me and taking me very slowly up my well-lashed arse. He didn't need any encouragement he just 'took' me as if it were his absolute right to do so, that was really cool.

Having someone as dominant and protective as Tyson made me feel very safe and, as a result, very bold. I found myself behaving in ways I would never have imagined myself doing before. For instance, whenever we go out to clubs, I will always dress very, very provocatively and stick my bum out as much as I can when dancing for all the men to ogle. Occasionally, I will go back across the dance floor to where my master is standing and kiss him, just to show them all who I am with. I know I am turning them all on with my cock-teasing performance but, with the exception of one very polite and brave guy who actually dared to ask Tyson's permission to dance with me, none of the others had the balls to try it on while my man was standing there looking so wonderfully mean and moody. It's like I have a sign round my neck letting the world know I am his property.

I've never felt that way with any white man I've ever met. Incidentally, Tyson was so surprised and impressed by the guys gall that he let him dance with me the rest of the evening. He does admire guts, it's a real warrior thing with him.

Usually, anyone who dares come near me will be dealt with very severely. Everyone knows I am Tyson's 'bitch' and wouldn't dare trying it on. I remember once, for example, another black guy who tried chatting me up in a pub while Tyson was at the bar conducting some of his 'dodgy' business dealings that I really don't know about and don't want to know about. Anyway, when he saw what was happening, Tyson came over and didn't even say a word. It was so cool. He just took the man's coat which was draped over the back of his chair and walked to the door and threw it out onto the street. The man didn't have any choice but to go out of the pub and retrieve it from the gutter. By the time he got back the moment had gone, and he looked pretty silly anyway so there was not much he could do about it. Tyson had made his point without saying a word or striking a blow!

At clubs, where he is invariably known and welcomed, I am encouraged to dance very provocatively for the benefit of all the guys standing around. On one occasion a guy I knew was a 'somebody' was at the club, he—like a lot of other guys—had been ogling me on the dancefloor all night. I'd seen him before, but what I didn't realise until this particular night was that he was someone whom Tyson was in 'business' with and their relationship had become a little 'strained', shall we say, for reasons that Tyson wasn't going to share with me—though intrigued I knew there were some things best left unsaid between us. Fact is this guy looked like he was brute and even Tyson admitted that he didn't want to mess with him—he wanted me to instead!

Whatever it was between them, it turned out that he was willing to call it quits with Tyson, if he could see me 'privately' for a while before he left. Tyson said a blow-job would probably be enough, but it was my choice should it go further, no pressure. Though I knew I was being pimped out like a hooker, in this context, I was a willing participant, found him attractive and was already feeling very horny anyway. I told Tyson to tell him I was willing to be his slut for half an hour. Tyson seemed mildly bemused that I so quickly acquiesced, but I could see that he was sort of relieved too.

About twenty minutes later Tyson took me into a room that I guess served as an office for the club, I figured it probably wasn't the first time it had been used in this way either, probably by Tyson himself, for that matter. After he left, within a couple minutes sure enough, in walks this guy who close-up looked bigger and more intimidating than I'd realised. A tingle hit me between the legs and up into my stomach. He said nothing, just presented me with his already erect cock and nodded down. We fucked hard on the desk in the end—after a little oral-sex! Afterwards he just said, "maybe I'll see you again?" leaving me his card. I just smiled and said, "We'll see". It was the situation that made it sexy at that particular moment in time and also the relative anonymity, it could never have quite the same 'rush' the second time around. Needless to say I didn't call him, but saw him a few weeks later with a younger blonde 'trophy' girl—the sort footballers go for, you know fake everything!

I know too many white women in my position who are walked all over. The guy will show up at their place for a fuck and even bring his mates, expecting the same. Never have any money. Thankfully, Tyson isn't like that. In a way, the relationship is one of mutual abuse. He uses me but, at the same time, I am using him. Even though I like being used as a sexual plaything occasionally, it's completely at my discretion, some girls get the wires all crossed and end up being totally abused—but not on their own terms. Having said that though, if that's what a girl actually 'wants', then that's quite a different matter. For my part however, being in control and maintaining it, is the key to my own submissive behaviour—if that doesn't sound too contradictory!

You see, after six months together, he still doesn't know where I live, and he never asks. He has no interest in my world or my friends or what I do. He is content to let me call him every few weeks, when my 'need' arises. Likewise, what he does or who he fucks between times is no concern of mine. This arrangement suits us both. It lets me explore other 'playmates', for example, because though Tyson is always an exhilarating lover, and will indulge and really enjoys some of my kinkier masochistic desires, I know his limitations now.

I've recently met this guy who has his own dungeon, and isn't one of those fake 'scene' creeps like I mentioned earlier. He's older, Peruvian and has this mystical, almost 'Zen' type vibe about him. He exudes a natural dominance that is without any noticeable trace of ego—an unusual combination making him quite unlike anyone I've ever met, and I'm expecting—when I've figured if I can really trust him, something like—and may be I am being overly optimistic—some kind of trans-formative, quasi-religious experience! To give over that much power though, I've learned it has to be done very carefully, but my instinct tells me he's good, and worthy of the 'prize'.

Chapter 11: Shayala

Age: 31, Location: Quebec, Canada

A mistress I had gotten to know at scene parties, Princess Sheeba, had decided it would amuse her, and be instructional for me, if I had some training from a master. Up until this point in my training I had only served female dominants. I must admit, the reason for this is that I had always felt more comfortable and safe with women. The idea of submitting myself to a man excited me, of course, but terrified me at the same time. Princess Sheeba told me this was a challenge I had to face in my journey toward complete submission. It was she who arranged for me to have a series of sessions with a master friend of hers. I did not know when or where this session would take place or with whom. I was instructed only to wait and respond. It was not until several weeks later that the call came.

I arrived home from work to find a message on my answering machine instructing me to arrive at my new master's home, by taxi, at seven o'clock the next evening. He told me to wear the clothes of my choice and to bring a bag with nothing inside other than black, patent pumps and black, sheer stay-up stockings. He did not want the annoyance of garter straps. He wanted me completely available without the slightest encumbrance. He reminded me of his intolerance for tardiness. In his opinion this was sloppy behaviour indicative of a flippant mind. The training of a slave, he advised, was not a frivolous endeavour and if I aspired to be worthy of such a process then I must show him the seriousness of my intent. He called this respect. I called it subjugation.

It was evening of the appointed day. Fifteen minutes to seven. I was standing on the west side of the Avenue du Parc wearing a conservative blouse, a very short skirt, black lycra leggings, and my ankle boots from Berlin. From my left hand hung a bag complete with the requested contents. I still didn't even know his name.

Admittedly, I was starting to worry. Normally, taxis roam this avenue frequently. Normally, it would not matter if I were a few moments late. Tonight there were no taxis in sight. And tonight, it mattered greatly if I were to be even a few seconds late. Irritation settled upon my spirit and a wave of anger rolled through my stomach as I anticipated his blatant complacency at my being late. I walked to the corner deciding that, since he would most certainly interpret my lack of promptness as having dilatory intent and thus harshly discourage my so-called 'oppositional' nature, I might as well buy a cigarette and enjoy the next few moments of comfortable laxity.

I stopped a taxi and scrambled in, spewed out my destination to the driver, and muttered a hollow "thank God" to the headrest in front of me. A faint smile passed over my lips as I smugly appreciated that he would have to find something other than my arrival time to reproach. It was six minutes to seven and I was right on schedule.

I entered through the unlocked door. He appeared at the top of the stairwell. A violet velour bathrobe covered his physique. He exuded a strong, silent and supreme poise coated with sensual indifference. I shyly responded to his casual "good evening" as I climbed the stairs and approached this commanding man who informed me his name was Sir Karl. Then something unusual happened. My spirit was brushed of its resistance and I felt a strange personification of apprehension, deference and obsequiousness. I found myself in front of him, staring at his feet, absent of any armour. In a whispered hush I uttered, "Good evening, Sir Karl."

He ordered me to undress and watched closely as I obeyed. He caressed me as he pleased. He invaded me as he wished. It was obvious from the outset that he regarded me as an inanimate object, existing solely for his use.

Many things were inflicted upon me that night; humiliation as he called me his slut and bound my body in defenceless positions where my anal and vaginal orifices were openly exposed for his pleasure; pain as he ignited my flesh with multiple sharp and cutting lashes from his collection of whips, paddles and crops; solitude as he abandoned me in a closed room while he enjoyed a candlelight dinner of chicken; pain once more as he twisted, pinched and pulled at my nipples; tenderness as he consoled me in my discomfort; pleasure as he placed me on the dining table, lined up three chairs, put each of my legs on the outside chairs, positioned himself in the middle and ate my sex as an entre'; frustration as he secured me on a cold seat, with legs spread, in front of an arousing erotic film and delayed permission to orgasm; humiliation as he ferociously thrust deeply into my vaginal hole and muttered what a good whore I was and then came all over my face with no respect nor remorse; protection as he allowed me to share his bed for the night and kept me close in his arms; and worrisome apprehension as he told me that I was going on a journey the next day, alone without him, to a place where I would learn how to embrace servitude, integrate submission, abandon my covetous nature for control and experience the pride of docile subordination for my Master, Sir Karl.

I awoke the next morning to the taste of a tender kiss and the touch of fingers tenaciously stretching the opening of my hole. He reminded me of the voyage. I told him that I was afraid to go alone. He replied that this was unimportant. Then he fucked me with his hand until I thrashed to exhaustion. My Master then fed me and left the house to pursue solitary interests for a couple of hours. Just before leaving, he recommended that, at two o'clock, I was to be ready to leave his house with my bag packed. He told me that he presumed I would be silent and still in the lounge, naked except for the garter-less stockings and pumps. I knew that he also expected me to be wet. I felt angry and unimportant, taken for granted and trivial; bored and nervous. However, I was grateful that he allowed me my mobility in his absence. A feeling of insurrection transiently tickled my flesh and I entertained the idea of fleeing his abode. Something warned me not to. The door slammed. He was gone.

At two o'clock sharp, Sir Karl came home. I realized that I had missed him and was longing for his touch, even if only on his terms. He seemed pleased at my obedience. In fact, so was I. The reward of subordination was becoming familiar to me and one that I had started eagerly to anticipate. I wondered if he would like to know this and was about to ask permission to speak when he shoved a finger in my cunt to inspect the degree of my obedience. He praised me and told me to turn my ass towards him. I did as he bidded.

As he kneaded my ass-cheeks, he observed that there were no marks showing from last nights play, adding that there was, therefore, all the more room for new ones today. He helped me with my coat and told me we were leaving. I know he saw the look of fearful anticipation in my eyes. Again, this was utterly unimportant. Once in the car, he ordered me to descend the front seat and lie back as much as I could. He placed a blindfold over my eyes, turned on the radio and told me not to speak, but just to enjoy the ride.

It seemed to me to be a long ride. Eventually, the car slowed, the engine stopped, and my blindfold was removed. I looked around and immediately recognised my surroundings. We were at the lovely home of Princess Sheeba. Funny, this did not appease me. I had never been left alone with the Princess and had never experienced the sternness of her hand when the only object of concentration was me. A memory flashed through my consciousness. I remembered having asked her for a cigarette at her last party and I had, admittedly, used a rather informal tone of voice. It seems I may even have forgotten to address her in the correct manner. With obvious disdain she informed me that she was Princess Sheeba and that I must never address her improperly again. She tossed a cigarette on the floor, just out of reach and turned her back on me. I was ashamed at my indiscretion and stunned at her severity. Would I see this stern severity again today? And if so, would the sternness flow this time from the crack of her whip?

Sir Karl rang the doorbell. In futility, I looked at him hoping that he would understand my covert plea that he stay. The door opened and we entered. Princess Sheeba appeared from behind the door in the most sensuous splendour. Her tight, olive skin contrasted seductively with the black netted material which barely covered her groin and exposed her perfect, rounded breasts. I was distracted by her beauty and momentarily forgot my anger at him for abandoning me. In fact, the fantasy of being permitted to finally taste and smell her womanhood aroused me to the point of forgetting that I was there to be trained. Sir Karl's manly voice interrupted the delicacies of my imagination. He ordered me to obey every word that the Princess uttered. He told me that he would be back in two hours. Princess Sheeba instructed me to wait downstairs. I heard Sir Karl tell her that if I did not obey she knew what to do.

My skin felt clammy. I wasn't sure if it was from the cold or from vulnerability. I waited, motionless, in the basement. Princess Sheeba said goodbye to Sir Karl. The front door closed. The basement door opened. Princess Sheeba stood poised at the top of the stairs. She looked delightful and seemed to survey me with equal admiration. But I felt ashamed and exposed.

Princess Sheeba gently brushed the hair off my shoulders and brought the black leather hood close to my face. She whispered into my ear that I was about to experience something that I had never known before. She told me that all I had to do was let go of my apprehension and I would feel the epitome of pleasure. She told me to trust her. I was afraid. She told me not to be scared. And then there was nothing but music and darkness.

Princess Sheeba began to wrap something warm and soft around my entire body. The warmth soothed me while the bondage disconcerted me in equal measures. I was completely immobilized and at her mercy for everything. She told me to lean back, but my body was frozen. She encouraged me to trust her. But still I hesitated. She firmly took my shoulders and ordered me to fall back. Reluctantly, I obeyed and she supported my weight to the floor. She told me that I had been brought here to be initiated into Dreamland; that I was finally ready. She told me that I should be proud to receive this honour. But instead, I felt like a fallen leaf, blowing alone in the wind, at the mercy of forces greater than I, with nothing familiar to settle upon. She asked me if I was okay. I replied, "Yes, Mistress". She told me that I was to address her as 'Princess' at all times. She would call me Gabriella.

Princess Sheeba began what she called the 'meditation'. Cutting through the powerful background music, her voice spoke to me with a hypnotic seduction. As I listened to her sensuality, I succumbed to her influence. Bit by bit, she relaxed my body and my mind. The leaf was now a feather and had softly settled on the ground in a warm spot protected by the base of an enormous tree. I felt safe. The Princess used her voice and the music in such a way that within a short time I had abandoned my body and was free of its usual sensations. She then entered my mind. She brought me to a place full of all my friends and family. The most important person in my life, my sweet love Luc, was also there. She suggested that I talk to everyone but she warned me that they could not see me, nor feel me, nor hear me. I wandered around the room, watching and touching everyone, feeling completely free because I knew they could not sense me. I felt that I could do anything, be anything, and no one would know. I did a somersault and landed in Luc's lap—he didn't notice. I kissed his lips—he didn't move. I fondled his groin—he never so much as flinched. Then I tried to go inside his body and feel every part of him.

When I tried this, I lost myself so I re-emerged into the room. Princess Sheeba told me that Luc was deeply in love with me. As I heard these words, I realized that I did not have to protect myself from the powerful emotions I have for him. I realized that my feelings for him could never be a passing occurrence. A warm breeze touched the inside of me as I recognised the love that I have for him. For the first time this recognition did not scare me. I felt the strength of spirit to travel to the raw roots of this love and not to turn away until I had done so. I remember gasping as I realized how very deeply I loved him. It was hard for me to imagine that anyone else could feel what I was feeling.

Suddenly, Princess Sheeba informed me that a new person had

entered the room. Her name was, apparently, Shayala. She told me to study her and to create her as I wanted to be. She was tall with long, blonde hair, robed in leather. Her skin was soft and very smooth. I liked her. I wanted to talk to her. But I was afraid, so I stayed on Luc's lap. Princess Sheeba announced that Sir Karl had also entered the room. All at once, I saw him. He moved very gracefully across the room like a panther. He strode confidently, but respectfully, towards Shayala. She smiled, turned away from him and immediately bent over with her ass high in the air. It didn't seem that she was afraid of him. Nor did it seem that she was angry. It seemed, instead, that she was there for him. He softly touched her ass and reached underneath her bent body to squeeze her breasts. He, too, was in leather. They stayed like that for a long time. The buzz of voices in the room continued, everyone oblivious to this strange scene. He caressed Shayala's wet mound and spread some of her juices to her anus.

Then he forced his finger into her ass and whispered that He was going to stretch her so that he could fuck her in the ass. Shayala wriggled her ass as indication of her submission. Sir Karl pushed his groin into her. Shayala moaned.

Princess Sheeba informed me that it was time to merge my persona with this girls. She guided me over to Shayala and prompted me to walk inside of her. I did so without the slightest hesitation. I wanted to be Shayala. I wanted to live submission the way she had in my mind. I wanted to feel subservient without feeling subjugated. I wanted to serve without feeling compromised. It was suddenly clear to me that he had brought me here for this. He wanted me to experience submission in a way I never had before; in a way that would release me from inhibitions, fears and threats; in a way that would heighten his pleasure and mine; in a way that would bond us eternally. And, as I became Shayala, I felt the emancipation. Princess Sheeba then guided Luc towards Sir Karl and the two personas fused. Suddenly, I felt his finger in my ass, and I began to eagerly anticipate being anally penetrated, maybe even violated. I was excited to serve him. I felt capable of enduring increased pain and interpreting it as pleasure. As Shayala, I was ready to obey, without rebellion, whenever it suited him; however it suited him. I had truly become a slave.

Princess Sheeba asked me if I saw her in the room. At first, I hadn't. When the Princess pointed out her presence, however, I saw a bright yellow aura surrounding a magnificently exquisite lady. She was utterly statuesque; a reigning beauty. The aura slowly dissipated and Princess Sheeba emerged. She was elegantly perched on a golden throne, powerful, mighty and goddess-like. I wanted to touch her. The Princess told me that I could approach the throne respectfully. As I did so, her legs parted. I could see the glistening fur of her pussy and my mouth craved for her taste. Princess Sheeba advised me to keep approaching and to kneel down between her legs. I could smell the sweet scent of her wet womanhood. The Princess ordered me to lick. I saw myself on my knees, with my ass in the air, and my head buried deeply in her groin. I could taste the indecent gormandise, yet, I could not taste enough. Princess Sheeba then told me that Sir Karl was behind me, ready to fuck my hole. I was to keep licking while he used me for his pleasure. The last thing I remember was feeling his cock in my sopping vagina and tasting her juices on my hungry tongue. At this point the meditation ended and I was brought back to the basement by the sound of scissors snipping the wrapping around my heated body. Princess Sheeba ordered me on my knees. She then informed me that I was to sample various instruments of pain and that I was to choose the ones I preferred. This way, I would be prepared for the next stage of my training with her. During the meditation Princess Sheeba had suggested that one could control the experience of pain through the mind. Now, she wanted to see if I had learned anything. She began with the first of eight instruments. My ass felt the cracks and lashes and blows of all of them. I selected three for future use—Mona's riding crop, Princess Sheeba's New York whip and the purple suede whip. Indeed, the pain had not felt as agonising as it could have. Maybe I had learned something more than how it would feel to have my head between the Princess' legs.

Then Princess Sheeba left the room for a moment. When she returned, I felt something cold on my ass and inner thigh. She asked me if I knew what was in her hands. I did not. She told me that it was her ice penis and proceed to insert it into my vagina. This was very uncomfortable but I managed to endure the painfully cold sensation. I was rewarded with the sound of a vibrator that found its way between my legs. Princess Sheeba commanded me to lie on my back while she tied my legs open with the bar. She shoved a dildo into my hole and continued to vibrate my clitoris. Simultaneously, she ordered me not to thrash in orgasm; that I could control this as well. I felt the heat building in my cunt and started to writhe. She kept commanding, "Don't thrash, don't thrash." I was losing control and felt my arms flailing. Suddenly, I peaked and rolled over on my side, aware that I had moved much less than usual. I was surprised that I had obeyed even with something I did not think was voluntary. I wished that Sir Karl could have seen this. I wondered if he would have been pleased with my efforts at complete compliance. The Princess left me to rest for a few moments. Then she raised my body to hers and took me into her arms. She held me tightly and welcomed me to Dreamland.

She removed the hood as I rubbed my eyes. I saw a big pair of black shoes by my knees. I looked up and shrieked in pleasure at the sight of Sir Karl. He had, it turns out, witnessed the whole process. He got down on his knees and I fell into his arms, never wanting to leave the shelter of his embrace. As Gabriella, I wanted to tell him how I was now. As Shayala, I wanted to show him the extent of my newly found uncompromised submission.

The profoundness of this experience is inexplicable. It continues to affect me, even weeks after. I have not seen Sir Karl for a while. And yet I know that he will provoke in me the new freedom that Princess Sheeba creatively cultivated within me on that cold Sunday afternoon. My love for Luc has probably never been stronger. The fears of emotional involvement have not been eradicated. However, I now have a new strength with which to confront them. This strength comes in the form of a bond that was fortified in an enchanted place called Dreamland; a place where, through the most exquisite abandon, I accepted him as my master and him as my lover.

Thank you, Princess Sheeba and Sir Karl for taking me to Dreamland and where, with graceful submission, I remain.

Chapter 12: Elizabeth

Age: 26, Avon Representative, living in East Midlands, UK

Like many other children I was bullied at school, but unlike other kids, I enjoyed being singled out and humiliated. I grew up in a city in the Midlands and lived in a multiracial area. I never knew my father and my mother was a well known slut. I always knew I was different as I was drawn to very aggressive boys at school and pre-ferred dating black boys because they were always horny. There was always something I was searching for, though I didn't known what it was. Even horny boys didn't excite me, and kissing and cuddling was a big turn off for me.

When I was about seventeen, I started wearing thong style panties and would pull them up extra tight between my legs and loved the feel of them cutting into my pussy. One boy said to me, while he was having a feel around, that my panties felt like rope. An idea came to me to go out and buy some rope and tie it around my waist and then through my legs and pull it up very tight so I could feel the thrill of it when I was out walking. In fact, I often climaxed in this way. Eventually, I even stopped going out with boys altogether, preferring to use a dildo on myself through the rope.

I still never knew my real self or my true needs and was well over eighteen when I got hold of a magazine with an advert for nude models wanted in Manchester. As it said that experience was not required, I thought I should give it a try. I phoned up and the man on the other end asked me if I was shy. I said I wasn't. He then asked me if I spread wide. I said I did. He arranged for me to come up the following Saturday. When he opened the door, he just said "in" and held the door open for me. Once inside, he then said "strip". I did as I was told and, even though I was wearing ordinary panties, the marks still showed from me wearing rope so tight. He then asked me if I was into bondage. To avoid the embarrassment of admitting to my rope knicker fetish I replied that I was. He informed me that he loved bondage and brought out lots of rope and leather wrist cuffs and collars to show me. I'd never seen anything like this before, but was very deeply excited when he put them on me. He pulled down the background material and there was a large black painted cross with steel rings to which I was soon tied fully stretched to. I cannot put into words how I felt, but a deep thrill went though me and my breathing came in gasps. I was tied and vulnerable in front of a man I had never seen before. However, my excitement was even more intense when two more men came in and starting talking dirty to me with very humiliating remarks. As the lights flashed on the camera it just blew my mind and I knew right then that this is what I was needing all along. I was placed in many different positions and it was all very exciting. With three dirty mouthed older men working on my naked body with rough ropes and rough handling, my brain couldn't take all the pleasure. I was still living it weeks later. And to think I got paid for having so much pleasure was a bonus!

There is no need to tell you that I went back to Mr X several more times. He told me on my last visit that another man was interested in me and that this man had a dungeon. I begged to meet him and Mr X said he would phone him. He did call later that night and told me the new master was interested in using me. I guess it was his use of the word 'master' that gave me a kind of tingle that I had never experienced before.

An appointment was set up at Mr X's house and I found that the new master was a Japanese gentleman. He took me with him to his place. As we drove along in his car he never spoke to me until we got to a large detached house with bushes in the front. He drove right into the garage and told me to get out of the car. He then led me into the house and told me to strip and watched me closely as I did so. He then took me down into the cellar where there were all kinds of ropes and pulleys and a large cage. To cut things short, I was placed in bondage and suspended by being pulled off the floor in positions that were very strenuous and more uncomfortable than painful. In fact, every position I was in was uncomfortable but very enjoyable and my mind went blank just taking in the feeling of pleasure. At first, I had the fear of falling but, as time passed, I gained confidence and the pleasure got so high I felt I wanted to feel pain to bring me down to earth. I was hung in every position and each gave me more pleasure. Pleasure is the only word to use here because there is no word that I can use to describe my inner feelings. This master could reach into my body and mind and could stretch them all at his will. He never said a word or explained what he was going to do. It was as though he knew how I felt.

I spent the whole weekend either bound or in the cage. Food would be brought and I was only allowed water to drink. I had to eat and drink from the floor of my cage. If I needed to go to the toilet there was one in the cellar and a shower too. The time passed so quickly. Of course, I couldn't see daylight or night time and there was no clock to look at and my mind was going into a blank. I didn't know the weekend was over until the master took me back upstairs and told me to get dressed and go. I dressed as I was told and then taken back through the garage to the car. Another man sat in the drivers seat and it was he who took me back to the railway station. He never spoke a word the whole time, but when we arrived at the station he handed me a note written by my Japanese master informing me to be back at the station the next Friday at 8 pm for another weekend in the cellar.

Had the master spoke to me about it before I left I could have told him that I could not make it the next weekend as much as I wanted to. As there was no phone number and I didn't even know the address, there was no way I could get in touch with him. Then it came into my head that Master X must know his phone number. I called him but there was no reply. He was either out or working on some other bitch. I tried all that weekend but to no avail. It was not until the Monday that I finally got in touch with him. I explained it all and Mr X said he would pass the message on. That evening Mr X rang me to say that there was no way the master would have me back and neither would he as he was now living with another bitch!

Shock and horror was my reaction. I felt drained. I felt that what had put meaning into my life had been snatched away. I had to stop myself many times from ringing Master X and the only comfort I had left was in meeting other masters to whom I could give myself. They could do what they wanted with me because this was the life I wanted now. Strange how things come about because I went to the nearest sex shop which sold specialised books and magazines and found a book about bondage. As I turned the pages it showed pictures of oriental girls in suspension. I noticed the pictures had been taken by Japanese photographers. The book was from the United Sates and too expensive for me to buy so I put it back on the shelf. I decided then and there that I would have my nipples and clit pierced and tattooed like the Japanese bitches and then I would save and go to Japan. But when I checked the air fares I realised it was going to take me a long time to save up and all the tattoo artists I approached could not do Japanese text. They told me to find a Japanese artist but so far I haven't located any here in Britain. I have never found another Japanese master either.

Since that first experience I have done a lot of bondage and been with masters of many different nationalities like Africans, Jamaicans, Greek and Turkish. Most just want a good fuck rather than bondage and really haven't a clue about it, but I can tell you that those African men can fuck for hours and be so rough. I need very, very aggressive, masterful men and have had many fucks with three men together and sometimes more than three. I still do nude posing for dirty men for fun mostly. I put adverts in contact mags and travel all over the place to meet men who want to strip me and be vulgar with me. Why do I do it? Well, I an searching for someone who will replace my Japanese master and who will take me as his total slave. Then I will be bound for better things!

Chapter 13: Jessica

Age: 35, Ex-Model, living in New York, USA

I've been told by many, many men that I am a very pretty girl and yes, I am blessed with all the right 'attributes' that make a girl very sexy to a man. But, as a girl, I have always believed this to be a line all men use to get inside a girl's pants. Of course, in my case, it usually worked since I love fucking. I have loved fucking ever since I lost my virginity when I was only thirteen years old. I was eighteen when the truth really hit me and I realised I was a nymphomaniac. Six months later I found out that, not only was I a nympho, I was a hard-line masochist as well.

It happened this way. One evening I was in bed with this guy (I don't even remember his name now, he was just one of many guys I used to pick up in bars), and I was on top of him with his cock way up inside of me. He had me lean forward until my nipples were brushing through the hairs of his chest, and he began spanking my ass. Each slap of his palm against my bare buns became a little harder than the one before it. Ordinarily a girl will tell the guy to go easy when the pain really begins hurting, but, and here's the weird thing, the harder my ass was smacked the more turned on I was getting. When I finally had my orgasm it was one of the wildest I had ever had, and afterwards I realised just how hard he had been hitting me because my ass was sore the rest of the evening.

After that first session of being spanked while being fucked, I began trying out things on myself at home. At first it was simple things like clothes pegs on my breasts, then on my nipples, and on down to my pussy. I would roll over on my stomach with clothes pegs all over the front of my body, press myself into the mattress as hard as I could so the pegs would hurt me even more when they twisted and pulled my flesh. And while the pain was coursing through my body, I would reach down between my spread legs until I found my clit, and masturbate until bringing myself to another of my wild orgasms.

After my first experiences with S&M and the knowledge that through pain I would experience far better climaxes than through normal intercourse, I sought out only men who were willing to do things to me that would hurt me, especially to my breasts, nipples and pussy. At first this was quite challenging as I didn't know how to go about telling a guy I wanted him to cause me pain when all he wanted to do was normal fucking. It was finally through a web site where dominant men were seeking submissive women that I began to find men who were really able to get into the pain thing. But, like most submissive women, I found that these men, even though wanting to be dominant, were almost all just the opposite. They seemed almost afraid to do things to me without my telling them what they could or could not do. Even when I told them they could do whatever they wanted just as long as it didn't cause any scarring to my body, they were still quite nervous and apprehensive about the whole thing.

And then I met the man I thought would be my life-long master. I had gone to a club by myself for an evening of fun and games, and was sitting at the bar having a drink when this guy came up to me and ordered me to follow him. He didn't ask if I would like to go into one of the S&M rooms with him, he simply told me to get off my fucking ass and follow him. And to my amazement, I did.

For the first time in my life I had found a man who didn't ask, but did as he damn well pleased with me, but he also knew not to do anything to me that would cause me permanent body damage. That evening I was whipped so severely on my back and buttocks that they actually bled. You would have thought I was being killed if you had been in the room with us from listening to all my blood-curdling screams. I mean Jim really laid the lash on me as hard as he could and no pleading from me stopped him.

He abused my body for almost thirty minutes without let-up. My nipples were pulled, twisted, and jerked.

Later, after one of the hardest sessions I had ever been in, Jim took me into one of the Fuck Rooms, complete with wall to wall mattress and cushions. He threw me down on my back (which added to my discomfort), took his own clothes off, and then fucked me like I had never been fucked in my entire life. It wasn't just a fuck, it was a wild fuck! Like I was being fucked by a man gone crazy. I had three orgasms with Jim before he finally came. This had never happened to me before. He then asked me if I would be at the club again next Saturday. My answer was that if he was going to be there, then so was I.

That next Saturday was the same as the first night with Jim. My ass, back, and thighs were whipped until I thought I was going to die, but that wasn't all! He then tied me down to a table with my legs spread out to each side in order to give him easy access to my pussy. He then took two leather thongs and beat both my pussy lips till they were completely swollen, then he stuck needles through them. This was another first and, I might add, a very painful first for me!

After we finished fucking Jim told me I was going to move in with him and be his live-in sex slut. Two days later I was moved in, lock, stock and barrel. Obviously, never been a live-in sex-slave before I didn't know what to expect, but Jim soon made me aware of what I could do, could not do, and what I would wear, and could not wear. The rules were very explicit. I was to take care of his every whim, wear only what I was told I could wear (even when at home), and fuck or be fucked when he wanted it. On top of that, I was to make my body available to whatever abuse he wanted to heap upon it. If he ordered me to lift my dress and pull my panties down so he could whip my ass, I wasn't to ask when, but to do it right away with no questions asked. I was also ordered to make myself available for sex and sexual abuse anytime he chose to bring his friends home for a little fun, using me as their plaything.

In fact, it was through Jim that I first got fucked by black men. Notice I say men, not man! One evening, he brought three guys home to the apartment for supper and I knew they were there for one reason only, and that was to abuse my body and give me a good gang-bang afterwards. Jim caught it all on camera again and loved watching me suck on their rods, one of which was particularly large and thick and, where the others just came in two or three jets, this guy seemed to be able shoot about seven or eight large shots of juice over my face and tits, like he was turning a faucet on and off. We joked after that he'd missed his true vocation and that he was more than a match for porn stars like Peter North, as well being much bigger to boot!

Jim and I had been living together for two years when one evening he sat me down and told me he was going to auction me off. I asked what the hell he meant by 'auction me off'? I'd never heard of such a thing. It turned out to be exactly what he said. I was to be taken to a very special club meeting where there would be other sex-slaves being auctioned off by men they had been living with.

Now you may say that I was quite naïve, but prior to this moment I really hadn't heard of this sort of thing, at least since they had abolished slavery in this country! But, as it turns out, it is not an uncommon thing in the harder end of the scene. When a master gets tired of the sex-slave he's living with, he can take her to an auction, sell her off and, if there is anything on show that he likes (that is, another slave-girl up for sale) he will bid on her and take her home to be his new sex-slave. Or he will simply trade what he has for what someone else has if they agree to it. Now, about the legality of such auctioning of a slave-slut. As long as the girl agrees to it, there's nothing anyone can do about it. And, as I found out, there's no sense in staying with someone who no longer wants you.

George, my current master, purchased me on the auction block that evening, and I have been his live-in slave for four and a half years now. He has asked me to marry him on several occasions, but for some reason I feel like if I were to marry him it would make him treat me differently and I don't want that. I prefer that things stay the same. He is a really great dominant and treats me very rough. He rents me out for gang-bangs at stag parties, and fucks even better than Jim used to. You know how some men tend to put their wives on pedestals, and I don't want any of that. I am a sex-slave and I want to stay a sex-slave for the rest of my life. Maybe someday I will break down and agree to marriage with George as I really do love him, but now isn't the time.

Chapter 14: Randi

Age: 28, Working 'Mom" living in Nashville, USA

There is nothing to compare with a woman's first submissive experience. No matter how many times she finds herself powerless beneath her master's hands, the first time she gives into the urge she's struggled with all her life to deny… that time she will not forget.

His name was Julian. And I love him still.

Over the years, I have become better at determining whether the person I'm playing with is a genuine player in the game of dominance and submission.

As a child I'd heard my father spank my brothers and knew all about the sound of a culprit being readied for punishment and the sound of the belt being flexed across the hand of the punisher. I remembered the silence before the whipping started and the quiet, shaky breathing of the victim steadying themselves for the first blow. And, finally, most terribly, I knew each crack of the belt would echo like a thunderbolt as it landed across the twin cheeks of the offending buttocks. I'd listened in fascinated horror as my brothers were led behind closed doors to face justice, knowing full well that when it was my turn, they would be doing the same.

When I met Julian, though, I was tentative, so uncertain of exactly what I was looking for that I wasn't sure I'd recognise it even if I found it. But at three in the morning, eyes dulled with lack of sleep and inhibitions at an ebb, Julian and I found our way together. I quoted, shyly, my favourite passage from an old book by Kathleen

Windsor: "Man belongs at the feet of God, and woman belongs at the feet of man". Disguising my hopes in intellectual discussion, I chanced that if he was offended by the implications of the quotation, I could claim it was the symmetry of the phrase that pleased me. But it wasn't only the words. And, in a matter of minutes, I found the 'S' to my 'M' and the tumblers of the lock that had stuck for so long clicked into place. We had reached a point of no return and both of us knew what would take place between us.

So we both experimented, testing our new roles. At a leather goods store, Julian picked up a riding crop and stroked it thoughtfully. I fidgeted nervously at his side, unsure of whether I was afraid he would buy it or afraid that he'd put it back. At a party, he came up behind me and wrapped his fingers firmly in my hair, forcing my head back against him. Neither of us ever talked about these tableaus, but I know he noticed the shaky breath I drew as he fondled the riding crop. And I know he noticed the way my body melted against his as he pulled me towards him.

One night, on the huge couch in the living room, Julian took me gently into his lap, wrapped his hands around my face and drew me close to him. "Now", he said seriously, "I want to see what you look like on your knees". For a long moment I stared into Julian's eyes before taking my place silently at his feet. He didn't say another word to me, but simply read his newspaper as he stroked my head absently. When he was through, he folded his paper carefully and, leaning down to tilt my face towards him, kissed me lightly on the tip of my nose. "Good girl." he said, "Now, without another word, put your shoes on and go home". As I drove home, one thought kept running through my mind: be careful what you wish for!

Two days later, I arrived late and Julian spanked me. I was reluctant and afraid, but Julian, ever patient, had his way (was there ever any doubt?). Of my own free will, I put myself over his knee and felt the unfamiliar, but long expected, shame and release as I received my punishment. I now know that the spanking was a mild one, but there were tears in my eyes as I rose from his knee. Julian never said a word. He couldn't find the right ones or maybe none were necessary. I'd either consent or I wouldn't. If I didn't, I could end the game. If I complied, I knew to expect more of the same. I complied (again, was there ever any doubt?).

In Julian's car I was stripped naked to the waist. He drove me through the car wash and the drive-up windows at the restaurant and the bank. I never asked permission to cover myself. When we got home, Julian took off his belt and punished me with no explanation. It was the first time he'd used anything but his hand. Also, it was the first time he'd given it to me on my bare skin. Afterwards, I slept in his arms. He stroked my hair and told me I pleased him.

For me, the road was an easy one. I had the need and he had the will. Female to male. Moth to flame.

His name was Julian. And I love him still.

Chapter 15: Clare

Age: 47, English Teacher living in Manchester, UK

I've always been attracted to brutes. When I was eight years old I was ordered to go out into the garden by my father and make my own switch for him to beat me with. My husband did the same. I'll always say to new boyfriends that if they don't dominate me, I'll destroy them. If a man isn't dominant or is too nice, I'll go for the jugular every time.

My most bizarre relationship within sub/dom was with a man called Morgan. He had been introduced to me by a woman friend called Vanya with the idea of us having a threesome. I had never been to bed with two people before, and it was something I was very interested in trying out. Vanya worked as an assistant to an inventor. She was the same age as me, but very curvaceous, statuesque, with a soft unlined complexion and boundless sexual energy which was hidden beneath her demure English Rose exterior. Morgan was forty four, very tall and slim, with thick brown hair and smouldering blue eyes. His love of sailing had the advantage of giving him a strong, supple, tanned body. He was a financier, well groomed and easily able to indulge his expensive tastes. Our first evening together as a threesome was a success, but that's another story! He nicknamed my pussy 'The Orange', on account of the colour of my pubic hair and possibly the juiciness of my fanny. I envisaged evenings of sexy fun but, although I realised he was a slightly schizoid character, I had no idea of the depths of his depravity.

At the beginning I was also totally unaware of the extent of Morgan's desire to control everyone in his life. Looking back, it must have been obvious to him that, although I appear as a strong, independent woman, I do have that need for domination. Though not, I must say, to the extremes he wanted to take me! Right from the outset our affair had a strange effect on me. There were several occasions when we met, ate a light meal with some good wine and made love for hours. Invariably, when we were at the heights of passion, I would start to hallucinate, seeing us in earlier, quite different lifetimes. Sometimes it would be medieval castles, more often we were sea creatures underwater. Of course, it was wildly exciting for me, and great for his ego to be having such an effect on me.

One evening he was very argumentative and trying hard to make me angry, but I wouldn't respond. All I did was to use calming tactics. Eventually, he became very frustrated with me and held my head, looking deep into my eyes. I just thought it was all very odd and quite unnecessary. He left early.

The following six weeks were to become a very strange vacuum in my life, because what he had just done was to leave me hypnotised. The only way I can be sure of this is because I used to keep a daily journal of thoughts and feelings to do with relationships. It was my safety valve from the somewhat bizarre lifestyle I was leading at the time. The sensation that pervaded during this six week period was of no longer having my own mind. I found I couldn't concentrate on my work as a freelance artist, or even cooking or conversation. He also, I believe, hypnotised and raped my lodger.

Afterwards, he told me that his reason for doing this to me was so he could use me sexually. This didn't really make sense to me at all because I was more than willing to experiment sexually anyway, only stopping short of extreme physical pain and injury. He had already brought his very pretty wife to me for a threesome, as well as his highly sexed young mistress, who loved him deeply and appeared to be his slave. So, even though I was prepared, indeed enthusiastic, to share in his sexual escapades, it still wasn't enough for him! I soon realised that he not only wanted to be stage manager, he wanted to be scriptwriter and producer as well! One way this manifested itself was to try to make me willingly have sex with people I didn't even find attractive. The worst example was a horrible old man who was in a coven locally of which Morgan was a member. He was very involved in witch craft which he used, not for spiritual good, but for power and making money.

While I was still under his hypnotic influence he continued to be a very dominant lover, but I found I was beginning to no longer enjoy the anticipation and enactment's of his domination. Previously, I had revelled in feeling helpless when he tied my wrists behind my back and then attached the same length of rope around my ankles. This was where his nautical knowledge of knots came in handy. He would caress and tease me by trailing the end of the soft rope across my most sensitive places with the implied threat of a whipping. But he didn't ever do more than give me a few light stings across my buttocks or breasts, just enough to cause arousal.

His sexy young mistress received more punishment than I did. I remember being taken out with them one lovely summers day on his yacht for what turned out to be one of the most exciting days of sex I've ever experienced. Boats, incidentally are wonderful places to have sex in because you can scream as loud as you want at sea and not have to worry about neighbours hearing. The most exciting of all was when we sailed along the coast, about half a mile out to sea, with his young mistress tied naked to the mast. He whipped her with a frenzy that was as frightening as it was exciting. And, all the while, sunbathers on the beach watched it all in disbelief.

He used to call me his 'lioness' because I prowled as I walked proudly along with my mane of thick red hair, animal reactions and instinctive behaviour. He liked the idea of having this wild creature fettered. For my part, the sensation of being completely at his mercy, unable to make any decisions for myself was a way of being a child again, not having to take responsibilities for my actions. I could act out the fantasy that he was my jailer and I had to submit to his lustful attentions in order to be allowed privileges. I wanted, and craved, to be used and completely filled up and overwhelmed by physical and emotional sensations.

As with everything, however, there was a price to be paid for this erotic adventure. During this period of hypnosis, I found myself turning into a shadow of my former self. All my usual zest and energy disappeared. It was as if I were merely going through the motions of living, like a sleep walker or a zombie. My closest friends noticed that I wasn't quite the same as normal, but it wasn't obvious enough for them to try and find out what was causing the difference. Although we still had sex, I couldn't remember much about it afterwards. My whole life experience seemed muted.

After six weeks had passed he staged another eruption of drama and crazy emotions for what seemed like a few minutes, and I was back to my normal self. He told me later that he'd released me from entrancement because he could only influence one lover at a time. Apparently, he now wanted to enslave another member of his harem. In any case, he said I was more fun when I had some resistance in me.

Sometime after that, he showed me some black and white negatives of a very plump man with an older woman. She was caressing a younger woman who was lying back with one leg in the air and an arm extended, obviously in the throes of ecstasy! He tried to convince me that the younger woman was me. I'm in pretty good shape for my age, but she looked a bit too slim to be me. The one element of doubt for me was that the extended hand was an exact replica of my own. I do have unusually proportioned hands. He had either been playing around with negatives, superimposing part of one image on another, or he'd struck lucky, or it really was me! Either way, I know he had been determined to exert power over me and use me in any way he chose against my wishes. At any rate, I had no recollection whatsoever of any part of the photograph, or his story. As you can imagine, it left me with a horrible doubt in my mind as to what I might have been used for. He had been trying to make me feel totally undermined, so I would have no certainty of who I was, or what I was capable of doing. Not surprisingly, I found all this extremely disturbing. It made me realise that he had no idea of what love is. He'd sworn undying love for me and behaved in a very loving way. But he couldn't help himself from using everyone he met, be it a business or sexual connection. He'd often blur the edges. I decided that any further contact with him would be far too dangerous.

THE END

If you enjoyed this book, you may also like to read the following sample chapters from other Magnolia Books all available on Amazon.

Other books from Magnolia

'Dominatrix (Vol 1): Candid interviews with 20 real life Dominatrixes' Compiled an edited by Roy Turner

'Submissive (Vol 1): Candid interviews with 20 lifestyle Submissives' Compiled an edited by Roy Turner

'Marquis de Sade: The man and his age' By Dr Ivan Bloch

Dominatrix (Vol 1) Sample:
Mistress Xena

Champion body builder, female wrestler and film stunt-lady, Xena was also one of the first female night club bouncers in Great Britain.

My mum thinks this is the safest job I've ever done; especially compared to when I was a bodyguard and was attacked on several occasions! She's quite happy with me doing this. As soon as I become jaded, I'll stop working. I have to enjoy it to do the job well. People will know if you're just putting it on.

I always insist on a detailed consultation to establish the areas a client's interested in; plus a medical check, as well. If they've got any problems like epilepsy or diabetes, for example, I need to know. I had a session just the other day where the gentleman passed out. I got him down into the recovery position and when I got him back he said: "Oh, I always do that". Now why didn't he tell me that before and I'd know how to structure the session and know what positions to avoid? Some mistresses are very conscientious, but unfortunately, some aren't. It's unbelievable the situations some people get themselves into knowing full well that the mistress isn't capable!

There are some very good mistresses in London. But, for people who don't know that much, they don't realise the difference. They might go and see some girl who's got absolutely no idea about safety whatsoever. They're just not trained up. I've heard of some horrible experiences from clients. I wouldn't even call some of them 'mistresses', because basically they're prostitutes with whips. I always tell the guys that the best way to find out if the girl is a real mistress is to ask her if she does sex. If they say no then they're a professional mistress and they're relying on their skills as a mistress. If they do provide sex then, in my eyes at least, they're not a professional mistress.

Talking about 'horrible experiences', I've known clients who've actually been blackmailed by mistresses! They threaten them with photographs, you see. I may take Polaroid's once in a while, but that's for the client if he wants a souvenir. But it will always be with discretion, it has to be. I've got one client who lives round the corner from my mum!

I know some mistresses who 'switch'; that is, they can be submissive as well as dominant. But for me that's never been a question. I've always been a dominant person in everything I've ever done. I've also known mistresses who've been slave-girls themselves. A lot if people think you can't be a dominant without also being a submissive, but I think you are either one or the other. Your mental capacity is for either being dominant or submissive, not both. Having said that, if it works for you then do it. But, for myself, I'm naturally dominant and that's it! I've always worked and competed on an equal level with men and very successfully, too! I've always been very good at every thing I do, and it's always been along with a more dominant role anyway. I was one of the first women night club bouncers in this country, as well as one of the first female body guards!

I've always been quite physical and I'm very confident in myself; especially with body guarding and door work. It's all about control. You're very aware of what you can do, if you have to. You'd much rather not, of course. You'd rather hold back and talk your way out a situation or deal with it in some other way. I think that's why I enjoy this work so much. It's fun! Or it should be fun. Some people take it so seriously, though. I've got a regular who comes to me once or twice a week just to do my house work and the gardening and so on. I'll put him into bondage and it's just fun. He's a nice person to have around. And he's got this incredible history of seeing mistresses for over thirty years; that's longer than I've been alive! To me, that's fascinating.

I've got 'domestic-slaves' who come here, too. They'll normally wear a boiler suit while they're working out in my garden, but they'll have always have ladies lingerie or something on underneath! If anyone sees them, it just looks like I've got a contractor working out there. They'll get a session at the beginning and another at the end, and they get the opportunity of long-term submission as well. I get a lot of businessmen who are used to being the boss themselves. I'll put them in a apron and a collar and order them around the day and they love it! It's because they don't have to think about anything. That way I always have my house clean, and I hate house work, anyway! Of course, if they misbehave, they're punished. That way, everyone's happy! If someone has a skill that they can offer that I need, I may consider them for service. At the moment, I've got plumbers, electricians and everything!

I only do about three sessions a day, and I'll spend about an hour and a half with each client. I prefer quality over quantity. And, besides, I do need some time to be able to sit down and relax between scenes. Because I do a lot of role play and I do wrestling as well, it can be very physically and mentally exhausting, so I need that time to myself. You find that you've just got a particular session working well and you've tuned into someone completely, and now you've got someone who is totally different! You can't keep that level of intensity up throughout.

I get so many clients from my web site these days. I spent such a long time setting it up and now it's just gone mad. I had a guy from Turkey with me yesterday. A lot of Americans, too. They come to see me from Heathrow Airport, which is only fifteen minutes away. They might only be in the country for a few hours, but they'll still come round, have a shower and a session between flights..

Every other person who comes to see me seems to be in computers these days, and they've all got access to web sites. I see so many different kinds of people; not just the high court judges, as people seem think. Everyone from corporate lawyers to postmen, in fact; that's why this has to be accessible to everyone who wants it.

Lots of accountants, too. I remember joking with one of the clients that I should advertise in Accounting Weekly (if there is such a publication), because I had one week where I saw about five accountants! I think it's because their jobs are so logical, and they can just go in and do it. Their brains just go off into this vivid imagination. And the same with postmen, because their jobs are quite boring as well, I think.

Remember, for a lot of people this will be the first time they've ever sat down and actually talked about these things! That's why I keep a lot of magazines like Domina around, because it's good to introduce people to things they've never thought about before. I've got a young carpenter who comes round and he always says he loves coming round to this house, just for the magazines! It's the fact that he can just sit down and read this stuff that is so great for him. I like to talk to people anyway (if they're nice, that is), so it's a lot of fun for me when they haven't seen something before; just to watch them discover something new is great! That's why I particularly love the sessions I do with beginners because everything is new to them. Sometimes it might not be what they're into, but then you move onto something else. There's always going to be something that will trigger them off. They've got no preconceived ideas about anything. I'm afraid you get some of the old guys, and they'll say: "I want this and I don't want to be tied like that". There's no element of surprise, there's just control right the way through the session. And I'm wondering, just who is the 'Top' here?

Obviously, because there is so much that can be done, I like to talk to them to find out what does interest them and what they do like and if there are any big 'no-no's'. If you do something in a scene like water sports, say, or electric's or something else that they really don't like, it can stop a scene stone-dead! So I need to know in a consultation what they're into. And that's why I give them a safe word, too. Fortunately, I'm very good at 'reading' people through working in security for so long. All of them are polite and respectful, though. One of my bugbears is uncleanliness. Long toe nails, too. I think it's disrespectful to the mistress, because a session can get very intense.

There are a lot of things I simply won't do. I don't cater for sex, for example; which actually really surprises a lot of people. They think sex is all part of it. But, as I said before, sex isn't something a 'genuine' mistress ever offers. I do allow leg and breast worship, but I don't allow oral service. It's just not hygienic. I don't do any cutting of the skin, either. But I will do 'safe' electric's. I enjoy 'enforced feminisation' combined with role play scenarios. Like, for instance, I'll catch a guy going through my clothes and I'll make him dress up in them! Making a man go around in four-inch heels is very funny because the tilt of the pelvis is so different. It looks quite uncomplimentary, too. So that's fun to do.

Then you've got the 'serial' callers. These are the ones who'll phone up and book an appointment with no intention of turning up. It's only through experience you learn these things. I've got a very good memory for voices. Everyone's got set key phrases or something that you remember. This should be treated like an appointment you make anywhere else but, unfortunately, they don't see it that way. Remember, I've put an hour or an hour and a half aside for these people, and I might have turned down two other genuine clients! One of the main pit-falls of being a mistress is that, because you're so involved in people's fantasy worlds, you're inevitably going to get a lot of people who write to you or phone you just to talk about it without any intention of showing up. It's just in their heads. That's why phone-lines are so popular; people can get their jollies without having to do anything about it.

Then you get the 'transit' ones who just go around from one mistress to the next. I've got regulars who will see me once a month or once every six months. I understand that it is a lot of money to some people. But it's more special to them, too. And I appreciate that and show it in the session by giving them my time and attention. For others, it's nothing. They can afford to come to me three or four times a week.

Different clients might like a different kind of girl. Some like skinny girls, some like bigger ones. In some cases, I'm not old enough for some clients. We all have our individual styles. Though I get a lot of regular clients, I might even see someone from another mistress as well. There are a lot of stunning older women working, too. You don't have to be young and pretty-pretty. To be honest, some of the younger girls are just too young. They don't have the maturity. And it's maturity that you need in this business, because it's about trust. You don't want some silly, giggly little 'girly'; it just doesn't work. It's all about suspending disbelief, really.

Because I'm a trained actress, I particularly enjoy the role-play. I've got an American police woman's uniform, that I'll wear for my Captain Hardass character. And I just love 'arresting' people! I've got one old gentleman who comes once a month and I always catch him trying to steal the television set! Actually, he couldn't even pick it up! As I'm a Black Belt and an ex-body building champion as well as a body guard, I try to show people different characters and let them know that there's more things that can be done in role-play apart from just the dungeon side. And when people realise that they think: "Oh, I think I'd like to try that next time".

One of my favourites is the 'kidnap' scenario; where we go out and pick up someone at an agreed point. I've got a couple of body guard friends who are ex-marines that I use as drivers. Sometimes I'll come in with a gun. If it's done somewhere quite public then I'll just come up dressed and take them off somewhere. What I do is I make them come here first and we'll talk it through, plus they need to sign a waiver just in case something goes wrong and the police become involved. We also take Polaroid's to make sure we've got the right person. In fact, I had a friend who was training and they had to do a kidnap off the street and they picked up the wrong guy, simply because he had the same hat on and the same jacket and he's pleading: "no, no, you're making a mistake!" They kept the poor man locked up for two hours before they realised! It seems ridiculous, I know, but it does happen unless you set it up properly.

I'm not interested in things like Chat Shows. The problem with Chat Shows is that they're only interested in the shock value. They're not interested in the lifestyle or the safety aspect or how nice the people in it are. There's a lot of humour involved, but they only want the sensational aspects. For me, this work brings together all the elements I've been trained for as an actress, as well as body builder and wrestler. I've even done a lot of fencing, which is perfect for crop work. I can use all these things to great effect. I never know what role I'm going to be called on to be next.

In fact, my first introduction to the scene was through being a night club bouncer. I was working for this one security company and they asked me to do this club night, and it turned out to be the Sex Maniacs Ball. And it was really lovely! The people were great and it was such a mad scene! Visually it was stunning. And I was being paid to walk around and watch it all happening! It was great! I can honestly say that, of all the places I worked in security, I found the fetish crowd were the best. There was none of the drug abuse or the selfishness or macho element you'd find in a normal nightclub. People were just getting off on what they were doing. What impressed me too, was the etiquette and the respect they have for each other. They would approach each other politely and ask: "May I play?" Those people who love to group everybody in as 'just a pervert' would find that amazing! In fact, other friends of mine that I brought in to do door-work with me, because I thought they'd be suitable, just loved it because the people were so nice and there was such a nice atmosphere. After that, I started doing more and more fetish clubs and met different people and went on from there.

Nowadays, I will occasionally take clients along with me to clubs if I feel they're suitable and I feel comfortable with them. People just don't realise what's available for them. Also, it's very difficult for people to get into the scene if they don't know where to go. It is coming out a bit now though. And there are the good clubs and the bad clubs. Some clubs are very big and, yes, you've got the play areas, but it is still a bit of a freak show for the 'other' people who are coming in. They may have the clothes, but not the attitude; and they know absolutely nothing about the scene. Then you've got the smaller, quality clubs where everyone's playing and everyone understands what's going on, which I much prefer.

At the end of the day, though, you need a life outside of this.

I'm lucky in that I've got friends who keep me grounded. I'm still involved in body building and martial arts training, so I've got friends from that. If I say to them: "Go and get me a drink"; they'll say: "I'm not your fucking slave". I'll say: "That's because you can't afford to be!" They purposefully won't do something I ask; where as, before I did this job, they wouldn't have thought twice about it! You need to take time out of it just to chill out and relax.

"Dominatrix (Vol 1): Candid interviews with 20 real life Dominatrixes' Compiled an edited by Roy Turner on Amazon from Magnolia Books.

Submissive (Vol 1) Sample: Janesca

Age: 36, Team Leader, living in Lincolnshire, United Kingdom

Though I am now a confirmed sexual submissive, nothing in my happy Dutch childhood, or very normal early sexual experimenting, even remotely hinted at the perverse pleasure I now take in my adoptive role. That knowledge was revealed to me in 1985 when I first came to live in Britain at the age of twenty one to do a years post graduate work. The knowledge so altered my life that I have lived, and loved, here ever since.

I appreciate that you're probably more interested in my sexual history, but that may be better understood if you know something of me as a whole person. You see, in my wider life there is absolutely nothing whatsoever submissive about me. I have always been a competitive sports person and a high academic achiever. My work environment is one of small, integrated scientific teams. My job, at present, is research work for a large international company. Incidentally, my HR manager commented that I hadn't operated at my best until I was appointed as a Team Leader. I say this not to boast, but to make people understand that in my normal life I am very assertive. Close friends, and non-sexual men friends in particular, have even criticised me in the past for being socially aggressive. Incidentally, this is something I refute as simply a cultural difference. It has nothing to do with my nature. Dutch women do not defer to males in the subtle ways most English women still seem to. All in all, nobody knowing me socially or professionally would recognise the persona I adapt to in a sexual environment. That persona is specific and limited to that particular sphere of activity.

A point I want people to understand is that my sexual behaviour is self chosen because this is what excites me. It is not because I am incapable of acting otherwise, or because of some long concealed psychological defect resulting from a childhood trauma. I like what I do, or rather, what I let others do. The thrill for me is the abnegation of self. I particularly like group sex where I become an object used without any consideration for my gratification. The first New Man who asks me what I want from a sexual experience would be very surprised and probably very hurt! I mean that I'm a very good Kick Boxer! I want to be told what to do, commanded, required to satisfy a man's needs. I like sex to be strong and raw and very potent. No pretence of gentle love. I don't want to be asked, because that involves me in taking or sharing responsibility for what happens to me. I want the selfish freedom of total obedience, of commands that give no option of choice and, as a logical extension of that, absolutely no guilt.

I want the privilege of saying to myself after a truly disgusting night, "Well, I was only obeying orders". That way one can indulge in the most debasing activity and feel totally humiliated, but wipe the slate clean of remorse afterwards with that as an excuse and motivation.

Okay, we'll start with me after six months in, well, let's just say somewhere in England. I had, by this time, got used to being chased by men in that curious amalgam of sexual crudity and courteous good humour that one only finds in this country. I attract that kind of attention a lot. I know I am exotically good looking. I am dark skinned with large brown eyes and long black hair. I am fine boned and rather small and petite. There were quite a few Indonesian imports into my family tree. The typical youthful Englishman's propensity to treat me as some exotic but, essentially, dim-witted doll was seriously counter productive and I resisted all attempts at seduction with little effort.

My studies threw me into contact with Vernon, a man in his early forties. Here was a quintessential Englishman, I thought. A tall, lean, supercilious iceberg on the outside, with a volcano hidden within. He was always polite and thoroughly correct in a work environment, but forever holding an invisible shield between himself and any real involvement. In a rare social moment I allowed him to know I might like a little less formality in our contacts. As a consequence, he kindly threw a small party for me on my birthday. I repaid him by getting slightly drunk. He had never, by word, look or gesture, indicated any interest in me as a woman. A sexual woman, I mean. This intrigued me. I wondered if he was queer. He bought a stone bottle of 'Zuidam' Jonge Genever—a particularly refined Dutch gin, especially for my benefit. The beauty of those bottles is no one notices how much one consumes. I consumed a lot and became inquisitive. I inquired why he had never made a pass at me. Didn't he fancy me?

We were sat on the stairs. He was one lower than me. Our heads were level. He admitted that, of course, he fancied me. I asked why he had never tried his luck? I can still remember his soft laugh when he explained the reason. He admitted he had, as he put it, strange tastes that would revolt me. The kind of games he played would not only revolt me, but hurt and frighten me, too. He told me that, in his games, he liked laughter at the beginning, tears in the middle and loud cries at the end. Those cries may be of satisfaction or of pain. With the kind of women he liked, there apparently isn't that much difference.

To this day I don't know why I pressed the point. I'd never had any great interest in him as a man. For a start, he was too old for me. And I certainly had never imagined any involvement in the kind of activity he hinted at. Sadomasochistic clubs are an accepted part of normal sexuality in Holland. I can't even pretend his words unleashed any secret desire. It was just what's often been described as my bloody mindedness that made me respond with a calculated challenge. "I thought you were supposed to be a scientist? You shouldn't theorise without evidence. Why don't you conduct an experiment?"

In answer, he leaned over, I thought to kiss me. I lifted my face. He asked, in a whisper, if I really wanted to? I nodded. He put his mouth to mine. His hand came up and cupped my breast. I grew a little breathless and then suddenly pain lanced through me as he bit my lip hard. I went to draw away, but he held me. His teeth slackened, and then his fingers found the nipple through the thin material of my dress. He laughed into my mouth as he felt it harden and then he began to squeeze with vice like fingers. Every girl has done that to herself, sometimes let a girlfriend do it. But this was more agonising than anything I'd experienced before. He whispered again in my ear, telling me all I had to do was ask him to stop. However, in my mind the challenge had been set, the gauntlet thrown down, and I would not ask. Instead, I let him continue till, at last, his own aching fingers gave way. Only then did I cry as the blood rushed back into the constricted knot of flesh. But I still watched him steadily through my tears.

Have you ever noticed how ice cool eyes can suddenly become hot anticipating orbs? He lifted his glass to me and jokingly punned that perhaps I was looking for Dutch Courage in my drink. I giggled and told him that it was rather Dutch Fear, in my case. None the less, I agreed to carry on the experiment and meet him in private that next afternoon.

Before I go on to describe what resulted from that gin lubricated talk, let me just add this. Many people, like me, will have had a conventional religious upbringing. This results in adding to sins attraction, but leaves one rather prone to guilt. Some of my internal disquiet was reduced a few days later by hearing a cleric mouthing in the wake of a tragic murder and rape. He was counselling calm to the bereaved relatives, but I felt he could just as easily have been talking about me and my situation.

He was asking why such things happen? Why a powerful being submits to such awfulness. Why not resist it? Stop it? I will tell you! Because nothing is so powerful as submission! How better to prove strength than by refusing to exert it? Overcome power by bowing to it. How better to exert ultimate superiority than by controlling one-self, not others? A willing submission denies the tyrant his triumph. Recall the story of the turned cheek. Who was the stronger? The striker or the struck?

I felt I had a spiritual sanction for an action I felt oddly com-pelled to see through. I approached that first meeting with trepida-tion, rather than excitement. No more than an intellectual curiosity and a childish sense of daring. Imagine my confusion to find not one man there, but two! Vernon sensed my nervousness and laughed, assuring me that, while he was peculiar, he was wasn't queer! His friend, Raymond, was someone, apparently, who shared his inter-ests. And he meant, quite literally, shared! He informed me that what I was prepared to offer him, I should offer Raymond as well.

In my innocence I was relieved. My initial response had been that a third party might provide some restraint. It did, but not in the way I had thought. The restraint would be applied to me, but I'll come to that in due course. I also felt, I must admit, the first stirrings of excitement. Raymond was much closer to my own age. Less than thirty, very handsome, and with an engaging smile. I liked that smile. He smiled a lot that afternoon, especially when I cried. Strangely, I was made to feel that everything that was done to me was somehow justified as long as he smiled.

Vernon was very clever, and very patient. To this day I don't know if he magically imposed a new persona upon me or merely revealed one that already existed deep within me. What I do know is that I experienced, for the first time, the phenomenon of what I call 'my other self'. It was as though another being took over my body. The 'I' retreated into a quiet corner and became an observer, not a participant. An observer making rational comments that this 'other self" had no wish to hear and, for the most part, ignored.

Initially, I was required to make the running. On the coffee table there were books and magazines dealing with flagellation. Vernon suggested I look at some and discuss them. The condition was that with each new volume I picked up I would be required to remove one piece of clothing. There was an odd, humiliating excitement gradually becoming naked in front of two fully dressed men. As concerned talking about the activities described in the magazines, I knew little and what I found was, I admit, mildly shocking. Looking back on that afternoon, I came to appreciate how fortunate I was to have such considerate mentors in the disciplinary arts. A more brutal introduction would not have inflamed me in the way it did. In fact, not until I had actually begged them to do anything, did either man attempt to really hurt me or physically control me. It all began with the mind games.

They could see what disturbed me in the magazines I flipped through and they made me talk about them. They asked me to imagine myself in the position described or pictured. They asked how I thought the girl felt. They required me to describe how I thought I would respond in her place. As I say, they were clever. Whenever that line of questioning got too much for me, I would toss that volume aside and select another, sacrificing an item of clothing in the process in order to avoid disturbing questions, so they won either way! They also made it clear that I was free to leave at any point. In fact, their cleverest ploy was to suggest several times that I do just that. Naturally, this only made me more determined to stay!

To cut a long story short, discussions soon turned to demonstrations. I was required to request each man in turn to spank me. I found it was not unduly painful, but neither did it physically excite me. In fact, I noticed another peculiarity about myself. In these kind of situations I seem to develop an incredibly high pain threshold. No, sorry, that's not quite accurate. I feel the pain, of course. I weep and cry out at it, but I don't somehow have the limits I would have in normal life. I can, and will, endure almost anything I am commanded to. What that first spanking did for me was to create an intense feeling of childish humiliation that ended up bringing me close to orgasm. My responses were more emotional than physical. I found myself seeking their approval and wanting to please. They interspersed the spanking by making me stand or kneel or crouch in various provocative and blatant poses, which I also found very exciting. They would then make me masturbate and lick my fingers one by one. Made me put my wet fingers up my arse, then lick them again. I found myself actually begging them to resume the spanking. Only when I pleaded 'nicely' enough, did they do it.

In fact, it was me who suggested to them that my introduction wouldn't be complete without experiencing the strap and the cane. However, Raymond felt that this was too advanced a step, considering my inexperience. He felt that I would not have the self control required to submit and would need to restrained. Of course, this was another clever trick on his part. Naturally, as soon he said that, I couldn't be denied, and he knew it! I found myself dissolving at the very thought of being helpless and at their mercy. The more they warned me that I wouldn't be shown any mercy, the more idiotically I insisted they should carry on. It was a very bizarre scenario! There was me pleading with them to be tied up and thrashed, while they both warned me in graphic detail of what they intended doing to me!

In actual fact, in comparison with later developments, they were fairly restrained with me. I had to choose who was to apply the strap and who was to wield the cane. I selected Vernon to strap me as my mental picture of Raymond with a cane in his hand had a 'phallic' symbolism all too perfectly understandable to that quaking, hidden rational self.

I wept a great deal. Both men used me sexually; my mouth, my arse, my hands, but never my vagina. They filled my sex organ with their fingers and tongues and various toys. A cucumber even played a part. But they never used their cocks, which further degraded me. Although I was deeply stirred, I didn't climax at all during the whole event.

Raymond drove me home that night, after about four or five hours of play, because by then I was in no state to make my own way. I invited him in for a 'coffee', leaving him in no doubt as to my ulterior motive. He ended up staying the night. He was very gentle, yet very ardent. The sex then was the best I've ever had. In fact, I was the animal, not him. I was insatiable and very noisy. I wanted the world to know how good it was. It's been like that with me ever since. I find that I rarely peak while actually playing games, but am primed for a long orgy immediately afterwards.

After that first session, it was left to me to suggest further meetings. They became quite regular, one or two a week sometimes. I was constantly bruised. They would invite one or two other men along, as well as the occasional submissive girl to join me for punishment. Some three months later, they took me to my first 'punishment party'. There were about twenty men there, as well as two other girls. It was harsh and unremitting, with the men spurring each other on and a new one taking over as soon as one flagged. I found myself being subjected to more pain than I would have imagined it possible to bear. There was also a strange feeling of sisterhood amongst us fellow female sufferers. Without any verbal agreement, we each knew when a girl had momentarily reached her limit and initiated strategies to divert attention. Sometimes we would actually claim her place at the whipping post out of 'jealousy'.

Strangely enough, there wasn't an awful lot of sex going on at these events, except for a lot of cock sucking, which I found degrading, but in an oddly delightful way. The ultimate humiliation was in being raffled, along with the other two girls, to see which man would have us as his bed mate for the rest of the night. I both resented and gloried in that. As it turned out, the man who won me was a useless lover and no help to me in my urgent need. I was still boiling when Raymond came to collect me in the morning. I made him pull off the road at the first opportunity in order to give me the good screwing I so desperately needed by this time. We fucked for an hour in some muddy field before I had calmed down enough to resume the journey home. Once at my place, we went straight to bed and stayed there for the next thirty six hours!

At the end of my years study there was no question of me going home to Holland. I found work in England and continued to see Raymond, but rather less of Vernon. It was an odd relationship, but very satisfying, in it's own way. We never socialised in the ordinary sense. I found my own circle of friends for my normal social life. As he put it, my time with him was strictly cock and cane! Amongst my fellow submissives I developed a taste for lesbian love. Naturally, outside of the disciplinary circle I became chaste. This was done both out of choice and necessity. After all, how would I ever explain to a 'straight' lover all my bruises and scars? In any case, sex without the preliminary stimulus of degradation and pain had lost its saviour. I had proved that to myself when I once persuaded Raymond to come away with me on a weekend trip. Without the element of discipline it proved highly unsatisfactory for both of us. We drove home early on the Sunday morning and never tried that silly experiment again!

As I understand it, I'm not required to give a 'blow by blow' account of my induction into the masochistic world. For this I'm grateful. Any woman who has been so regularly whipped will tell you that the experience becomes a blur. Only the observer differentiates the time, the tool used and the savagery or artistry of the user. For the receiver, there are only two points of reference. Those are the flood and ebb of the pain and the voice of the Master. It may encourage or denigrate, insult or praise, but one listens to that voice with greater attention than to the whine of the descending whip.

What outsiders fail to appreciate is that the submission game, like sex itself, although apparently a bodily function, is in reality a shadow play in the mind. What happens on the skin only serves to supplement what goes on in the psyche. I have discovered that to submit is the greatest liberation of all. Restrained and 'helpless' under the whip, I have a freedom few women ever know. A conventional woman, no matter how excited, either through self interest, love or just courtesy, still considers her lover's feelings. Massage his ego, compliment his technique, admire his physique, wilt under his stamina, praise his virility. All this and yet still maintain an image in his eye that will grace his table.

As a submissive, I have no such obligation. I can be utterly, selfishly absorbed by my own feelings to the exclusion of all else. All I have to do is obey my Master's command and accept whatever he chooses to do to me. Paradoxically, as a masochist, I have no obligation to make an effort to please him. In fact, he is, quite literally, pleasing himself, and me, using my body as the vehicle. For my part, I can simply focus my energies on returning to that pain filled 'sweatiness' that is our common genesis. I can sweat and fart, scream and weep at that most fundamental level that civilisation strives so hard to deny us. There is an incredible primitive pleasure in screaming that has nothing to do with the degree of hurt. It is simply a release of, and from, everything.

For example, I have frequently been made to piss myself, either as a reactive, that is, relinquishing of control due to excessive pain, sometimes even of pleasure, or simply from being kept in restraints for a longer period than my bladder can sustain. Once I even shit myself and was cruelly whipped for it. I carry the scars to this day. But where a 'normal' woman might carry long memories of shame at such ill treatment, my shame is immediate and profoundly satisfying. It's also forgotten the moment my shackles are removed. Nothing that happens to me under duress (however secretly I permit or desire it) is really my responsibility. Basically, from my point of view, he did it and he made me do it! At the price of a little temporary pain, I'm freed of any limit to my most indulgent and primitive desires.

We females are closer to our genetic inceptions than men, both in body and in mind. The process of our monthly bleeding reminds us both of our designated function and our relationship to the animal kingdom. Men try to distance themselves from this. Only men could create a religion that denies sex its pivotal role and asks its priests to remain virginal. The ancient female religions celebrated nature by having its priestess's play the whore and give themselves to worshippers on the temple steps, thus celebrating the gift of sex in congress as close to the altar as they could get. My whippings strip the 'sophistication's' from me. I can't pretend, I can't pose, I can only be… me!

Anyway, back to my story. I was promoted at work, which meant I had to move home. I was overjoyed professionally, but desperately worried about how it would affect my 'secret life'. Raymond simply shrugged his indifference and, a week later, informed me that he had 'transferred' me to a new master in Lincolnshire who would allow him visiting rights. I don't know how to explain the strange gratification I got from the knowledge that I had been disposed of like a slave at an auction!

During the flurry of moving and the resultant hiatus, I had a brief, mad interlude of a marriage to a kind, but straight, man that lasted less than six months. We parted without bitterness. It was a mistake. I still use his name though, which is why I can reveal my maiden name. Anyway, I soon returned to my old ways of sexual servitude as Raymond had decreed. I am still with that master; actually, a duo of masters! Two brothers. Within the restricted confines of rural Lincolnshire I meet both of them quite often, both professionally and socially. By convention, our exchanges have to be limited as they are both married. As I'm still in my thirties and considered very attractive, I am naturally an object of suspicion amongst the local married women. I know there is a rumour going around in local circles that I'm supposed to be gay. I've done nothing to foster this, but neither have I gone out of my way to deny it. I find it takes the pressure off if they can pigeon hole me in some way. However, my looks still ensure that I'm frequently included on invitation lists, so I'm frequently meeting my masters outside of the disciplinary context.

There is a piquancy in maintaining a nice balance of friendliness and formality when out in public with a married man who, perhaps only a day or two before, had me hanging by my ankles while he whipped me between my legs as I sucked his cock. Him refusing to stop beating until I had sucked him dry, and me, if in a playful mood, not sucking hard at all, knowing he preferred my screams to my tongues caress. Or I may give way to the temptation to lightly bite instead of suck, and thus stimulate him to vicious revenge.

The anomalies imposed by this odd mixing of the private and public worlds can produce strains that need tempering by an understanding friendship. I am very fortunate that within a year of moving to Lincolnshire I met someone at a Whipping Party in Nottingham who I recognised as living in the same village as me! We became confidants, friends and then lovers, in a comfortably muted fashion. My friend is also a kind of submissive, but more of an observer than participant, so neither would or could stimulate me in the way

I require. Our bedding is more friendly than fervent, the only kind of lover who not only doesn't object to my bruises and cuts, but is secretly pleased and excited about them. I have to say nice things about Jan. You see, I'm dictating this. It's actually Jan who's doing the writing. Thank you, Jan, darling! No, of course, that's not his real name. It's a joke between us. We share the same name, as we share so much else. It's another way we exclude reality from our private world!

Lorraine

Age: 37, Location: Surrey, United Kingdom

My fantasies have always every time around sacrificial scenarios—with me, of course, as the more than willing victim! Sometimes, in my dreams, I am in Ancient Mexico being sacrificed to the gods by half naked, feather bedecked Aztec priests on top of a pyramid and under a cruel, merciless desert sun. Other times, the scene is a secret coven of pagan witches and wizards who spread eagle me naked on a cold stone slab before using me in their potent fertility rites.

In fact, my fantasies can get quite, well, fantastical! Like the time I am on another planet being examined as a scientific curiosity by alien professors. Even wilder; my tormentors are not even human, but many-tentacled triffid-like plants, prodding and probing my naked body.

Whatever the scenario, the main erotic ingredient that is ever present is the ritualistic element. There is always a definite theatrical structure to the proceedings that I need to totally involve me. Also, my masters/tormentors (the more the merrier, as far as I'm concerned!) Are always masked or hooded like executioners or medieval inquisitors to give them a frightening, dispassionate anonymity. No one speaks, apart from my master who may issue occasional instructions to the men. After all, they all know their roles in our erotic pantomime.

Above all, I am not informed of what I am letting myself in for at any session, nor am I given a choice in the matter. My present

Master, Matthew, works on the assumption that if a scenario excites me as a fantasy, then there is no reason he shouldn't 'force' me to do it for real. Looking back, I realise that if I had not been forced into situations without any option for refusing, I would probably still be the sheltered, naïve little housewife I was when we first met.

Perhaps I should explain the whole situation of our relationship at this point. You see, my Master is also my boss. I started working as a part-time typist and receptionist for his company two years ago. It wasn't long, however, before we realised our mutual interests and began an affair. My office duties now take on a very different meaning as you can imagine!

Anyway, this cover works perfectly for our regular 'get-togethers'. My boss/master can ring me at home at anytime when he wants me without arousing my husband's suspicions. I know I am a filthy slut, but I must admit I get incredibly turned on and excited if my husband takes a call from Matthew and relays the message in all innocence that I have to be at 'work' at such and such a time. The fact that only I know the true meaning behind the summons is very erotic to me.

If I answer the phone while my poor, unsuspecting hubby is in the room, Master Matthew will invariably take a cruel delight in giving me very explicit instructions about how I am to dress when I present myself for his pleasure and what sexual acts I will be expected to perform. As he talks dirty I have to maintain a business-like pretence, answering his lurid suggestions with "I'm sure that can be arranged" or "I don't see any problem with that" or some such innocuous reply.

The heady cocktail of guilt, intrigue and danger gets me tremendously excited even before he's laid a hand on me. Added to this the fact that I'm actually being paid an hourly rate by his company for all this (which is more than Monica Lewinsky was!) Makes me feel a real horny whore.

On one particular occasion my husband had taken the call while I was out screwing another lover (but that's another story; not even my Master knows about that one!). When I got home I was feeling well-fucked and (I thought) fully satisfied. But when hubby informed me that Matthew had called saying he had some 'very important' clients coming for a meeting the following Tuesday evening and he needed me to offer hospitality I knew that this was going to be the big one I had fantasised about! As far my poor, deluded spouse was concerned the job meant nothing more than making the sandwiches and serving coffee. I, however, was under no illusion that the only tasty morsel being served on the menu would be my naked body! Master Matthew knew all about my desire to experience a group of men together in a sacrificial scenario and had promised to arrange it as soon as he was able to gather together a suitably qualified group of helpers.

I could hardly wait for Tuesday to roll around. As each day passed my fear and excitement grew in roughly equal proportion until my pussy was literally permanently buzzing like a dynamo in anticipation of being well-filled and well fucked. On the appointed evening, I prepared a dinner for hubby to eat in front of the TV. My son Jason wasn't interested in dinner. He was going out, he informed me. He was very evasive and blushed coyly when I inquired where. As he has just turned eighteen I assumed he must have found himself a girlfriend and let the matter drop. Adolescents have their own secret world that adults are not allowed to know about, I reflected as I popped upstairs to get ready for Matthew. Still, I found myself grinning mischievously to myself, teenagers are not the only ones with secret rendezvous!

When I arrived at my Master's house I was taken immediately into a side room off the main hall. From the adjoining lounge I could hear masculine voices talking and laughing. It sounded like four, maybe five men. They appeared to be having a party. My stomach churned in anticipation of an out and out gang bang. Suddenly, every instinct in my body wanted me to turn and run back to the sanctuary of my safe little home and cosy spouse.

Master Matthew sensed my trepidation and frowned reproachfully. Despite my fears, I was more worried about displeasing my master than what might happen to me. Above all, I wanted to prove to Master Matthew, and myself, that I was able to offer myself up to his will completely. He reminded me of the fact that he was only fulfilling the fantasy that had come out of my own imagination, not his. And that I wasn't being forced to do anything I hadn't previously admitted I wanted to do.

There was no point denying it. Master Matthew had wrung every last erotic fantasy out of me under his interrogation. And I knew well enough what his rules were. Any fantasy can, and will, become a reality. In a frightened whisper, in case the noisy party in the next room overheard me and I might cause embarrassment to my beloved master with my inexcusable insubordination, I dared to ask how many men were waiting to use me. He just smiled that cruel smile of his and, cupping my chin in his powerful hand, turned my face up to him and informed me there would be enough to satisfy even a cock hungry whore like me!

I needed desperately to know what I was letting myself in for. I felt I had to prepare myself mentally for the erotic ordeal I knew I must face, but I knew he wasn't going to tell me. Ignoring my silliness over numbers and details, my master wisely ordered me to remove my coat, knowing the act of stripping would always get me in the mood for sex. With trembling fingers I unfastened the buttons down the front to reveal my complete nudity beneath-as he had stipulated I should arrive.

I felt incredibly excited, as I always did, as I felt his lecherous eyes ravishing my body and his big strong hands took hold of my ample breasts, squeezing them just hard enough to hurt a little and then bouncing them appreciatively in his massive palms as he weighed them like a pair of ripe melons. Next, his fingers expertly traced a line down between my cleavage and belly, and then across the freshly shaved smoothness of my pubic mound and slipped easily into the moist crack of my pussy.

Exploring the hot wetness, he grinned knowingly, "So, you don't want this, eh? We both know your cunt has a different opinion, don't we, slut?"

I blushed with shame at this undeniable give away of my desires and tried to avert my eyes from his penetratingly, powerful gaze. My mouth was as dry with fear as my pussy was wet with excitement. It was these conflicting sets of emotions fighting against each other that addicted me to our games and made me return to my Master again and again.

The question was repeated with greater insistence, interrupting the delicious delirium caused by his fingers probing roughly inside me.

"Yes." I weakly admitted, feeling myself powerless to do anything but be completely honest about even my most filthy and disgusting sexual needs with my Master. Master Matthew then ordered me to take off my coat and hang it up. Enjoying the sight of me stark naked in the hallway.

"The hour of your sacrifice has arrived." My Master announced with grave, almost religious, severity. "This is your moment of truth where you must prove yourself and the faith I have put in you as my most treasured slave. You won't let me down?"

I assured him I wouldn't. I was so anxious to prove myself a worthy slave by pleasing all his dominant male friends. My failure to satisfy them all sexually, no matter what they might require of me, would reflect badly on him and their estimation of his ability to train a slave and bend her to his superior will.

Next he draped the black velvet sacrificial cloak around my shoulders, fastening it in place with a heavy gold locket so that my nakedness was completely hidden beneath the heavy shroud. Then he put the leather hood in place on my head so that only my eyes and mouth were revealed, thus assuring my absolute anonymity. "You know what you must do?"

As if I could forget! I had fantasised my way through the pageantry of this scenario a thousand times in my imagination already. But I managed to conceal my excitement and merely confined myself to a simple, "Yes, sir. I know what is expected of me and I will not fail you."

He smiled at me as a father would upon his favourite child. I felt a glow of satisfaction that I might yet become his most favoured sex slut.

"Come, girl." He said soothingly, as he led me to the living room door. He made me wait outside, head bowed, while he went ahead and announced my entrance to the waiting men. Through the closed door I could just discern the muffled voice of my beloved tormentor informing them that their entertainment was about to commence. There were murmurs and grunts of lewd animalistic approval that sent shivers down my spine and put butterflies in my belly.

Matthew emerged from the room, after what seemed an age and, just before he led me in to face my fate, whispered in my ear that, although I wouldn't know who, one of his guests was well known to me. It might be one of my work colleagues at Matthew's company; it might even be my husband or father, he suggested with an amused air and an evil chuckle.

This was so typical of my Master to add such a cruel twist at the last possible moment in order to spice up the proceedings even more. My mind was suddenly flung into even greater turmoil at the thought as I found myself guided into the centre of the lounge surrounded by Matthew's special friends. It was too late for regrets or retreat now. There were six of them in all, not including my Master. They stood, lining the edge of the room around me. Each had a drink in his hand, and some were casually smoking cigars as they eyed me in eager anticipation of seeing my nakedness revealed. It might have been a very normal get-together, except for the fact that, apart from their executioners style hoods that my Master had specified they should don, they were all stark naked and sporting rampant erections!

With great ceremony my Master slowly unbuttoned my cloak and took it from me, leaving me naked in full view of all these strangers. Instinctively, I modestly cast my eyes down to the floor while my left arm shot up in an attempt to cover my breasts and my right hand went down to hide my pussy from all those lecherous eyes. Then, catching the disapproving look of my Master, I remembered my place and my role. Letting my hands drop to my sides, I drew myself to attention, like a slave on an auction block, fixing my gaze firmly on the wall ahead of me and tried desperately to ignore those lust-crazed eyes fiercely feasting on my vulnerable nakedness.

Soft, sensual mood music started to play on my Master's sound system. I recognised it from our previous one-to-one sessions and knew exactly what was required of me. Slowly and seductively, I began moving my arms and body in time to the music. Losing myself in my erotic dance, I swayed and twisted like a shameless strip-tease artiste. I had been well trained to perform this way and my Master often said I was a very sexy dancer for my age with my still trim figure, tight buttocks and firm, bouncing boobs. The only trouble was I had only performed like this in front of one man before—not a whole group of wanking males!

Still, it didn't take long for me to get into my perverted solo performance, and quite soon I was showing myself off to them all with pretty wild abandon while they closed in on me from all sides like a pack of hungry animals for a group grope. Wriggling provocatively as a dozen hands touched me up, I thrust out my pert buttocks and spread my ass cheeks with my fingers to expose my arse and wet pussy for inspection. As their exploration of my body grew wilder and more intimate, I did my own bit of ogling at all the cocks on display. Safe behind my mask, I enjoyed myself by grabbing any cock that came within reach as they rubbed up against me. I then dropped to my knees for a 'circle-suck', as my Master calls it, and proceeded to take all their throbbing pricks in my mouth one after another. I was both amazed and delighted at the variety of shapes and sizes on offer. I was getting very carried away now, particularly with one young man whose fresh, sweet-tasting cock excited me more than some of the other men's members. Even with their faces hidden, I could tell most were late middle-age or even older.

At a given command from my Master the men scooped me up into the air. Quite without warning I found myself held high and helpless, like a coffin, on their shoulders. They carried me aloft, like pall bearers, and headed from the lounge with Master Matthew leading the way. Again, I was both thrilled and terrified that my fate was being decided for me and I had no idea what was in store for me now; only that I sensed the moment of my real sacrifice to the Gods of Lust had arrived at last!

The adjoining double doors were thrown open and I was borne on high by my prospective abusers into the Master's dining room—or what I remembered as a dining room! For this very special occasion Master Matthew had excelled even himself with his attention to erotic detail by transforming the space into a veritable temple of sacrifice. The curtains were drawn tightly closed and the dining table itself was covered in a black silk sheet, like a pagan altar. Around the darkened room ornate candles cast ominous shadows against the walls. Incense burned everywhere, adding a final, almost mystic touch to the scenario. I could feel my pussy juices flowing freely and my nipples hardening to rigid nuggets at the exciting, yet terrifying, prospect of what was to become of me and finding that I was already so consumed with desire that I didn't even care anymore!

Slowly, gently, my exquisite tormentors laid me out on the altar like a prize offering to their cruel, unforgiving God of Lust. Silently and expertly, they spread-eagled my arms and legs, pinning me down by wrists and ankles. In doing so they made sure that they positioned themselves in such a manner that my fingers could still grip a pair of the hard cocks offered me, while my toes were in intimate contact with two sets of testicles! Next, I was stretched wide as each man in turn went down on me, licking and sucking furiously at my soaking cunt. Then my master demonstrated his skill at abuse by introducing some very interesting objects into me. First, a dildo, then a candle, followed by a long stemmed wine decanter and, finally, his fist. I could tell by the appreciative noises being made around me that Master Matthew's guests were suitably impressed by his skills as a dominant, as well as my threshold for this kind of extreme abuse—thanks, of course, to the wonderful training my master had already given me. I felt a warm glow of satisfaction and achievement, knowing that I was proving myself a worthy asset to his harem.

When my master had decided he'd had enough of this phase of my abuse, he motioned for each man in turn to have sex with me, while the rest kept me pinned down and spread wide. One after another, I was subjected to a thoroughly rigorous fucking by each of the sweating, grunting and abusive elderly men as my master stood back and surveyed the scene of debasement, playing with his own cock all the while and urging the others on to use my 'whore's hole' with as much force as they could muster and not be dainty with me. Meanwhile, several score of frenzied fingers continued to grope and maul at me mercilessly as I kept up my teasing of their cocks and balls with my own digits to make sure I kept them all at full boil!

Naturally, I was paying particular attention to playing with the youngest man's tackle, which I was gripping firmly in my right hand. Without warning, his excitement at seeing a woman, who must be old enough to be his mother, acting the part of such a shameless slut before his eyes, got the better of him and he spunked furiously, spraying thick white streams all over my face and tits. Greedily, like some whore possessed, I began licking at the gobs of sweet tasting boy-spunk still dribbling out of his cock and down the lovely thick shaft of his purple headed monster. As well as enjoying the act tremendously, I also wanted to ensure he got hard again as soon as possible. I was determined I was going to have that cock exploding in my pussy before the evening was over. I also had a sneaking suspicion my Master had something lined up for me and this young, novice dominant. As it turned out, I was right!

Master Matthew had indeed got it all planned out for me, as I knew he would. At his command the men let go of me and stood back, leaving me for the young stud to pleasure himself with. The horny boy didn't waste any time in taking full advantage of the opportunity or of me! Grabbing me by the legs, he dragged me down the table to impale me on his already hard-again cock. Then he proceeded to give me the fucking of a life time while the others wanked over me. Without taking his delicious cock out of me, he somehow managed to clamber onto the table and on top of me. There was no stopping me now as I wrapped my legs round his waist, locking him in position, and grabbed his firm young buttocks, urging him to thrust harder and deeper into me. I was like a bitch on heat and determined to put on a really filthy sex show to impress my master's guests, as well, of course, as making sure I got as much mileage out of this succulent young man as possible. My hands and mouth were everywhere, scratching his back and sinking my teeth into his neck and shoulders, leaving him covered in love-bites. The thought of being a cradle snatching whore was really turning me on! After fucking my cunt in a variety of positions, Master Matthew told him it was time to give my ass-hole the same treatment. Accordingly, my young lover withdrew his cock for a moment and, flipping me over, proceeded to ram himself into my arse right up to the hilt, at the same time reaching round to maul at my tits very roughly. There was no respect from this lad for a mature lady old enough to be his mother, which is just the way I wanted it!

He came several more times as we fucked on that table. Once in my ass hole, and another time in my cunt. Counting the first time I'd taken it in my mouth, that meant I'd had his spunk in every orifice. In addition, the other men, inspired by our antics, all shot their respective loads over me till I was covered in the hot, sticky stuff. Eventually, I wore out all their cocks and Master Matthew instructed them to pick me up again and carry me to the bathroom where I was to have the spunk washed off me in a most unconventional manner! Once there, I was ordered to kneel in the bathtub while each of the men took turns to hose me down with a good, hard pissing! Again, my master decreed that my young stud should have the honour of finishing the group urination with something special for their entertainment.

While the others gathered eagerly around to see what was about to happen, Master Matthew ordered the young man to stand in front of me and to, in his own cruel words, 'give the whore a drink'. I knew what this meant as it was one of the master's favourite ways of abusing his women. He produced a funnel, which he handed to the boy with instructions to shove it down my throat. For the first time I sensed some hesitation in the poor young chap which, I must admit, is a bit of a turn-off for any submissive woman. But I put it down to his youthful inexperience, and reckoned that with my master's expert guidance and encouragement, he would soon overcome his inhibitions. Thankfully, with the lewd encouragement of the older men, he finally managed to overcome any reservations he may have had about this act and went for it with gusto! Shoving the nozzle of the funnel unceremoniously into my mouth, he proceeded to let loose a powerful torrent of pee down my throat that kept me swallowing hard to avoid any spillage, which I knew from painful experience was a punishable offence in my master's eyes. The men cheered us on, delighted at this new, amusing way to abuse a slut's mouth and, I'm pleased to say, applauded me at the end as a good 'all-rounder' before taking their own turns to use me as their human piss-pot!

When it was over, and I had guzzled down as much piss as they could produce, Master Matthew suggested the group retire to the lounge for more drinks and, as he humiliatingly put it, "leave the slut to make herself presentable enough to be sent home to her poor hubby". I was left to my own devices in the bathroom to cleanse myself and try and regain some semblance of dignity while, next door, the men discussed me lewdly like a piece of meat.

I waited in the bathroom for more than a hour, until all the men had left. Now that the scenario was over and I was back to being my other 'normal' self, there was no way I wanted to face any of them. I certainly didn't want to see their faces unmasked, anymore than I wanted them to see me. Anonymity was the key to my pleasure.

As I drove home that night, I re-lived the excitement of that memorable evening, going over every delightfully sordid detail. I couldn't wait until my master summoned me for another session. Tomorrow, I would see Matthew at work, but I knew nothing would be said about tonight. His manner would be business-like and detached. And I know there would be moments when I would doubt any of this ever happened. That was the rules of the game that we both knew must be obeyed.

'Submissive Vol 1: Candid interviews with 20 lifestyle Submissives' on Amazon from Magnolia Books.

'Marquis de Sade: The Man and His Age' Sample: Fashion

Clothing! That can make women seem more desirable by showing just slight hints of charms and arousing the passions of both sexes. That is the rôle which Marquis de Sade had Minister Saint Fond impart to fashion. Saint Fond also recommended to Juliette that she should show herself half naked in the streets to the public if she wanted to remove her last vestige of modesty.

Here, too, de Sade let reality speak. The advice of Saint Fond was actually followed. "On a quiet day of the year V of the Revolution two women paraded up and down the Champs-Elysées, completely nude and covered only with a thin gauze. Many women also showed themselves with wholly base bosoms. The sight was not unusual."

The blaséness was shown in remarkable conceits. Young men and women tried to better nature and borrowed the white hair of age. The de Goncourts excellently describe the incessant changes in fashion in their bizarre fancies, their delicate concealment and unveilment, the gigantic *friseurs* of the women, their "make-up," beauty spots and patches, etc. Fashion paid homage to the age.

The nearer one comes to the time of the Revolution the more does nudity appear in fashion. The style of gauze, the preference for gossamer becomes more apparent. The clothing of the "Goddesses of Reason" becomes ever more transparent. Clothing retreated to the centre to show its opposite semicircles, bosom and legs. Ankle bracelets and golden rings on the toes were the fashion. Terpsichore, in the Greek fashion, reigned in the public gardens. A journalist who attended the opening of the Parisian Tivoli, declared that the goddesses appeared in such light and transparent dress that nothing was left to the imagination. "The women in the audience are dressed as outrageously as possible. The indecency of their behaviour is impossible to describe. In the last great ball in the opera house Madame Tallien appeared garbed only with jewels in the necessary place." These costumes, whose wearers were called *merveilleuses*, had been introduced in Paris by Therese Cabarries, the mistress of Tallien, after she thus publicly showed herself in the Reign of Terror in Bordeaux. The male *merveilleuses* were called *incroyables* and clothed themselves according to the ideal of offensiveness. For during the Revolution the highest ideal was not beauty but power and strength of muscles. Don Juan was changed to Hercules.

The perverse sexual impulses also found expression in fashion. The wide spread paedicatio, also practiced between man and woman, brought the notable fashion of the so-called "Cul de Paris." It spread to such an extent that even the prostitutes delighted in this form of passion, since it was the "style." Under Louis XVI the seat in women's dress was so extended that they resembled "Venus Hottentote."

On the other hand, tribadism was a cause of rather strange costumes. The tribades with male inclinations had remarkably increased during the Reign of Terror. The virago on the streets was a daily incident. Her costume differed little from the man's. Since her hair was cut close and her voice was strident, it took a good look to make sure of the sex.

Bordellos and Secret Pornologic Clubs

Marquis de Sade had made his studies for his two notorious novels *Justine* and *Juliette* in Paris. Here he, himself, experienced and conceived the greater part of the contents. Parisian incidents and experiences had permanently fructified his phantasy. And the models for the descriptions of individuals in his works are easy to discover. This will be shown in surprising fashion in the discussions of prostitution and sexual life in Paris. Even today Paris justifies the remark of Montesquieu in his *Persian Letters:* "It is the most sensual city in the world where the fanciest pleasures are invented." De Sade's description of the great bordello with its ingenious contrivances and settings refers almost entirely to Parisian bordellos. Most of his heroines are Parisian prostitutes. It is therefore fitting that we should cost consider these conditions.

In Juliette, (I, 87) the Marquis de Sade describes the bordello of Duvergier in a suburb of Paris. This madame had a bordello for both men and women. In a private house, surrounded by a pretty garden, Madame Duvergier had her own cook, delicious wine and charming maidens who received ten lounsdors for a *tête-à-tête*. The house had the requisite back entrance for safeguarding of propriety. The furniture was of the best; the boudoirs most fitting for their purposes. Duvergier, protected by the police, could celebrate more atrocities than her fellow-madames. The bordello supplied princes, nobles, and rich citizens with its wares.

When Juliette organised a house in Paris, six pimpesses (*maquerelles*) were sufficient to provide for girls from Paris and the provinces. Clairwil introduced Juliette, into the house of the "Society of the Friends of Crime," which lay in the heart of Paris but was discreetly concealed. It had splendid drawing-rooms, boudoirs, *cabinets d'aisance* and harems or, as de Sade called them, seraglios in which both sexes disported themselves in wild orgies. The girls were, for the most part, torn from their parents, under the protection of the police. Here the respectable world was assisted by hangmen, jailers, floggers and flagellants (Juliette III, 33 ff.).

Alcide Bonneau believes that the Deer Park served de Sade as a pattern for his descriptions of bordellos. Nonetheless de Sade had made a thorough study of Parisian bordellos and had found many incidents to his liking. He wrote (Juliette I, 333) that in many bordellos in Paris turkey-cocks were much esteemed for lustful purposes in zoophilia. At any rate it cannot be denied that de Sade took his descriptions of Parisian bordellos from actual experiences. Authentic reports will conclusively confirm this.

The most notorious bordellos of Paris, the secret pornologic clubs and the affairs of the prostitutes will be described in later sections.

The most famous, most sought after, most mentioned Parisian bordello in the Eighteenth Century was the House of Madame Gourdan on Rue des Deux Portes; under the reign of Louis XV and Louis XVI it served the court and nobility. This bordello was distinguished by the genteel attempt to satisfy every desire of male and female visitors. A short description of the place is appended.

1. The *"Seraglio."* This was a great salon with *"plastrons de corps-de-garde,"* i.e. twelve prostitutes who had always to be in a position such as to satisfy any whim of the visitor. There the price and details of their pleasure were agreed upon. Even the minute details were stipulated. Pidanzat de Mairobert at this description in *The English Spy* cries out: "Just imagine the horrors and infamies that took place in such a house!"

There is no doubt that de Sade expressed such a great preference for the word "seraglio" from this salon of Madame Gourdan. De Sade also discussed the understandings on the price of love in his novels and was particularly concerned with the analysis of the details for preparing an orgy.

2. The *"Piscine."* This was the bathroom of the bordello, where the girls, fresh from the provinces, were sent to the madame. There they were bathed, powdered and perfumed. Among the many essences and toilet waters was the famous *Eau de Pucelle*. This was a strong astringent with which Madame Gourdan renewed "lost beauties" and restored that "which can be lost only once." Marquis de Sade often mentioned this remarkable miracle which will be discussed later under the section: Cosmetics and Aphrodisiacs. Also in the *piscine* was the *Essence a l'usage des monstres*, which made impotent persons potent again by its strong odour and excited them to passionate cruelty. The specific of Doctor Guilbert de Préval (we shall later say more of this charlatan) was truly a magic charm. For

it served at one blow as a prevention, diagnosis and cure of syphilis! Truly a sexual panacea!

3. The *"Cabinet de Toilette."* Here the students of the Venus-seminar received their second lessons.

4. The *"Salle de Bal."* From this classroom a secret passageway led into the home of a merchant on Rue Saint Sauveur. Through his house the prelates and preachers (*gens à simarre*) as well as respectable ladies could enter the bordello. In this secret room were clothing of all kinds as well as "objects of delicacy." Here the clergy could turn into laymen, officials into soldiers, ladies into cooks. Here the respectable ladies permitted unflinchingly the powerful embraces of a coarse peasant, whom her trusty madame had chosen to satisfy her indomitable temperament. On the other hand the peasant believed her to be one of his own kind and was little embarrassed in expression and action.

5. The *"Infermerie."* This was the room for the impotent. The attendants tried to incite and arouse drooping spirits by all possible means. The light fell from above; on the walls were passionate pictures; in the corners stood similar statues; on the table lay obscene books. In the alcove was a bed of black silk; its top and sides consisted of plate-glass so that it mirrored and reflected all the objects and actions of this pretty boudoir. Perfumed thorny switches served for flagellation. *Dragées-pastilles* in all colours were offered for food; "only one was needed to make one feel like a new man." They were called *Pastilles à la Richelieu* because he had often given them to women as aphrodisiacs. Women were also taken care of in this *Infermerie*. There were present so-called *pommes d'amour*, little balls of stone, to satisfy them. Mairobert could not discover if "the chemists had analysed this stone which had a decided chemical reaction and was often made use of by the Chinese." The *consolateur* was an ingenious instrument "found in convents" as a substitute for a man. Madame Gourdan did a wholesale business with this artificial phallus. In her possession were numberless letters from abbesses and simple nuns asking her to send them a *consoler*. Great, black rings, so-called aides, served the men as artificial irritations in wom-

en. Many of these rings were covered with hard studs for increasing the pleasure. Finally there was a whole arsenal of *redingotes d'Angleterre*, which are today called condoms, and which, as Mairobert has it, "protect from the virus of love but dull the pleasure." Madame de Sevigné called it "protector of pain and despoiler of pleasure" in one of her letters.

6. The *"Chambre de la Question."* This was a private room in which one could see through a secret peephole all that took place. A contrivance for voyeurs.

7. The *"Salon des Vulcan."* In it was a *fauteuil* of a strange form. The moment one sat in it, one was snuck a heavy blow. The person sank backwards with outstretched legs, which were fastened to the sides. This chair was a discovery of Sire de Fronsac, son of the Duke of Richelieu, and served him as a faithful aid to seduction. The *Salon des Vulcan* was so situated that the crying and wailing could not be heard outside the room. This mechanization of vice will also be found in de Sade's writings.

Gourdan was the leading madame for the respectable world. She could satisfy all desires and was extremely wealthy. In Villiers le Bel she had a private country house in the forest to which she seldom went but often sent her sick and pregnant girls. The villa also served as a useful hiding place for especially delicate debaucheries. It was ironically called by the peasants the convent.

There were two kinds of *madames* in Paris; first, the seducers of virgins, second, purveyors of already deflowered maidens. Only the first were punished by being forced to ride backwards on an ass. Gourdan belonged to the second class and took care that her novices were officially prostituted by one of her assistants. But the head-madames had also to make regular reports of the physical health of their girls.

We shall later give such a report.

In the House of Gourdan the mistresses were educated for the respectable world. The later Countess Du Barry had to thank her resplendent career to her early stay at the bordello of Madame Gourdan. Many aristocrats also sought new pleasures here. A respectable lady, Madame d'Oppy, was discovered in 1776 by the police at Gourdan's where she was officiating as a prostitute.

On November 14, 1773, Madame Gourdan delivered a funeral oration on her deceased colleague, Justine Paris, which was printed in *The English Spy* and is so full of sadism that we append a short summary of it. The idea for this funeral oration was conceived by Prince Conti, one of the most notorious adventurers of the *ancien régime*. It was read at an orgy in Conti's home. The "Funeral Oration of the very proud and very powerful Lady, Madame Justine Paris, Grand Priestess of Cytherea, Paphos, Amathonte, etc. given November 14, 1773, by Madame Gourdan, fellow Priestess, in presence of all the nymphs of Paris" has the characteristic motto:

Syphilis, O my God!
Has put me under the sod!

On their dying-bed Justine's parents preach to her that immorality is the only redemption for the future.

"Don't count the days you haven't consecrated to pleasure!" Justine immediately transposed this advice into action, which one finds on almost every page in the novels of Marquis de Sade, and dedicated herself to the advice of her parents. She then entered a Parisian bordello, where she made great advances in the service of Venus and became famous through an affair with the Turkish ambassador.

Trips to England, Spain and Germany taught her to be phlegmatic with the Englishmen, serious with the Spaniards, and ardent (*emportée*) with the Germans. She finally came to Italy and in Rome was the "Queen of the World and the centre of *Paillardise*." She travelled through all Italy, honoured and coveted by nobles and clergy. Unfortunately she was attacked from time to time by her hereditary syphilis but that did not prevent her at her return to Paris from celebrating new orgies, winning success and great honour as the proprietor of a bordello. She ended in a hospital.

Could this funeral oration have been unknown to Marquis de Sade? It is hardly probable; it is almost certain that Madame Paris was the prototype for Juliette who was celebrated throughout all

Italy, in Florence, Rome and Naples as the queen of the world and as the ideal prostitute.

Casanova, the famous confidant, whose historic trustworthiness is attested by Barthold, told in his *Confessions* of a visit in 1750 to the bordello of Paris, the so-called Hôtel du Roule, and presented a living picture of the life and action in a Parisian bordello of the eighteenth century, which may here serve as an addition to the more systematic description of the house of Gourdan.

"The Hôtel du Roule was famous in Paris, but was as yet unknown to me. The proprietress has furnished it elegantly and has from twelve to fourteen splendid girls. One finds there all the desirable comforts: good table, good beds, cleanliness; her cook was excellent, her wine splendid.

"She is called Madame Paris, undoubtedly a pseudonym that pleases all.

"Protected by the police, she was far enough from Paris to be certain that the visitors to her place were persons well above the middle-class.

"The inside was well policed by servants, and all pleasures had a fixed tariff.

"One paid six francs for breakfast with a nymph, twelve for a dinner and double that for a night."

Here we pause for a moment and declare that the above description of Casanova tallies almost word for word with the description of Duvergier's in de Sade's *Juliette*. The house of Duvergier was just like that of Justine Paris.

Casanova died in 1798; his memoirs reaching only to 1773 remained in manuscript form long after his death and were not made public until 1822. *Juliette* appeared early in 1797. The only conclusion to be drawn is that both men have described independently the same bordello. To return to the description of Casanova.

"We enter a fiacre and Zatu says to the driver: 'To Chaillot.'

"After half an hour journey he stops before a gate on which is a sign, Hôtel du Roule.

"The gate was closed. A Swiss with a great beard stepped out from a side-door and seriously sized us up with his eyes. He found us respectable, opened the gate and we walked in.

"A one-eyed woman of about fifty years, but still showing traces of former beauty, greeted us and asked if we would like to dine.

"Upon my assent she led us into a very pretty salon, in which we saw fourteen young maidens who were all pretty and dressed in muslin.

"At our entrance they arose and made a charming bow.

"All were about the same age, some blonde and some brunette.

"Every taste could be satisfied here.

"We spoke a word to all and made our choice.

"The two chosen let loose a joyous cry, embraced us with a passion that was virginal, and we went to the garden expecting that we would be called to dinner.

"This garden was extensive and so arranged that it could serve the joys of love.

"Madame Paris said: 'Go, sirs, and enjoy the fresh air and reassure yourselves; my house is a temple of peace and of health.'

The Erotic Literature

The French literature of the eighteenth century is brand-marked pornography! At no other time in the history of the world, even under the Caesars, had literature been made a tool of vice in such a systematic fashion as in the ancien régime. Of course, the representation of sexual passion was an old story in French literature, and was even present in the numerous fabliaux of the middle ages; but it was not until the eighteenth century that the healthily coarse naturalism and naiveness of these older forms of erotic stories were replaced with pictures of sensuality, whose studied premeditation served as a malignant stimulus to an enervated society. The eighteenth century produced the greater part of the pornographic literature existing today; and in the number of individual erotic works more than all the other centuries combined. The lion's share in the production of pornography falls in the period from 1770 to 1800 when only eroticism could move the public. These books made the worship of flesh their main theme. They recognised nothing but lascivious experiences and all the forms of sexual pleasure. The bordello was a paradise, the prostitute far nobler than the most faithful wife. "What age has so dirtied itself with obscene books as this great century?" asked Janin, "that even men like Voltaire, Rousseau, Diderot, Montesquieu and Mirabeau fashioned their works accenting to the taste of the time." Shortly before and during the Revolution machlosophy appears to have suppressed all nobler motives. The bookstores were literally pornographic libraries. Mercier declared in 1796: "Only obscene books are displayed, especially those whose title-page and frontispiece mock and jeer at modesty and good taste. Everywhere these monstrosities are sold in baskets and pushcarts near the bridges, the doors of the theatres and the open streets. The poison is not expensive: ten sous a book." The principal market was the notorious Palais Royal, of which we shall later speak. This centre of all vice was also the principal market for the obscene writings that flooded Paris. One found these works even in the toilette rooms of Parisian ladies. Bernard has an interesting tale about this which also serves to show the enormous spread of the writings of Marquis de Sade: "A respectable lady both in age and position had written out a list of books she intended to take to the country for herself and children and asked me to procure them for her. On the list was Justine or The Misfortunes of Virtue, which she thought was a pedagogical work!" That such writings were plentiful in bordellos was not strange and, indeed, such is the case today. Napoleon I ordered all such books found in the possession of prostitutes to be seized and destroyed; only one example of each to be saved for the National Library where they we still preserved in a special corner of the building.

De Sade forever talked of obscene books. Juliette and Clairwil ransacked the dwelling of a Carmelite monk, Claude, and found a select library of pornography. Juliette said: "You have no idea what obscene books and pictures we found there!" First they note the Porter of Chartreux, "more a comic than a dirty book, which the author, nevertheless, is supposed to have written on his death bed." Second, the Academy of Ladies, well conceived but poorly carried out. Third, the Education of Laura, a wretched work which had too little vice, murders and gouts crûels for Juliette. Finally, The Philosopher Therese, the enchanting book of Marquis d'Argens with pictures by Caylus, the only one of the four books that combined vice and atheism. And the monk had, of course, a number of the "wretched brochures that we found in all the cafés and bordellos."

The Marquis de Sade, indeed, intended his works to serve as models for all later obscene works.

We present as an orientation a short survey of the most important French erotica of the eighteenth century. For a complete list die student is referred to Gay's Bibliography of Erotica (six volumes).

The Ovid of the Eighteenth Century was Pierre Joseph Bernard (1708-1775). In 1761 appeared his l'Art d'aimer, a verse imitation of Ovid's Art at Love. Nevertheless it caused great excitement and was present in the toilette table of every respectable lady. The verses were bound together with rose-bands and were appropriately about billing and cooing. But these latter were very passionate and the plainness of speech compared with Ovid. Bernard enfolded in his poem a whole course of refined sexual life, in which he recommended strongly the reading of piquant works.

The younger Crébillon (Claude Prosper Jolyot de Crébillon, 1707-1777) can be called the real creator of lascivious writings in the eighteenth century. His writings were characterised by an "elegant cynicism and graceful vice." The most famous was The Sofa, a Moral Tale, whose title indicates the content of the work. Of a similar kind were The Loves of Zeo Kinizal, King of Cofirons (1746), which described the love adventures of Louis XV; The Night and The Moment (1755), Oh! What a Story! (1751), The Sins of the Heart and the Spirit (1796), etc. In Crébillon's novels the tendency is apparent: to prettify and justify the commonest sensuality with a philosophic cover.

Jean François Marmontel (1723-1799) created the type of anticlerical novel in The Incas, and had unmistakable influence on the representation of the clergy in later erotic novels.

Sidelights on the History of M. Dirrag and Mlle. Eràdicée, in addition to the case of Girard (Dirrag) and Cadière (Eràdicée), portrayed the sexual debaucheries of the Jesuits. De Sade, as we have seen, ascribed this work to Marquis d'Argens and the pictures to Count Caylus.

André Robert Andréa de Nerciat (1739-1800) was for two years librarian in Cassel and was later confidant of Queen Charlotte at Naples. He wrote the notorious Félicia and a sequel Monrose or a Libertine by Fate.

That pornography at that time was fashionable and in good taste was shown most strikingly by the circumstance that the greatest figures of the age did not disdain the earning of this cheap fame.

We have already mentioned that savant of the classical times, Caylus. But such men as Mirabeau and Diderot did not shrink from sullying their literary work by the production of obscene stories. Mirabeau especially was often quoted by de Sade and there is no doubt that Mirabeau's Education of Laura served as the model for Philosophy in the Boudoir. In My Conversion Mirabeau described the experiences of a male prostitute, who had respectable ladies, nuns, etc., pay for his services. A third obscene book of Mirabeau's was Erotica Biblion (1783).

In Denis Diderot's Jacques the Fatalist were presented obscene stories that put him below Crébillon's class. His famous The Sister which, "when first published, was thought to have been written by a nun, dealt with the torture to which a nun was put by the perverse lubricity of her abbess, for whom, it was said, Diderot found a model in the Abbess of Chelles, a daughter of the Regent, and thus a member of a family which for several generations showed a marked tendency to inversion." (Havelock Ellis in Sexual Inversion.) His Indiscreet Joys was also erotic and contained a number of paradoxical assertions and paronomasias in the sexual field; this feature probably gave occasion to de Sade's preference for Diderot.

Choderlos de Laclos was the Petronius of "a less literary and more degenerate epoch than that of the real Petronius." His much quoted Dangerous Liaisons described the corruption of the aristocracy, of which the author, the friend of the notorious Philippe Egalité, has first-hand knowledge.

Less cynical in his description of the debaucheries of the nobility was J. B. Louvet de Couvray who drew the type of the "chevalier" in his Loves of Chevalier de Faublas. In Faublas' rich love-adventures the hero (borrowed from the artificial effeminization of the real Chevalier d'Eon) played a rôle also found at the end of Juliette where Noirceuil, dressed as a woman, married a man.

Next to the Marquis de Sade the most famous erotic writer of the Revolutionary period was the productive Restif (Rétif) de la Bretonne. We shall later evaluate Rétif de la Bretonne as one of the first critics of de Sade. We are at present interested in him only as a contemporary of de Sade and in his influence upon him. It was plainly Rétif, whom de Sade referred to unfavourably in his novels: "R... floods the public and needs a printing press next to his bed. By good fortune they groan alone under his frightful products; a dull decrepit style, nauseous adventures in the worst society; no other merit but a great verbosity for which only the store-keepers will be thankful." May not professional jealousy have played a pact in his judgment? We will later see that Rétif did not think much better of de Sade. It may also be that the highborn Marquis thought himself far removed from the lowborn Rétif.

Indeed Rétif de la Bretonne (1734-1806) mainly occupied himself with the representation of the moral corruption in the lower classes, thus supplementing the work of Marquis de Sade, with whom he had otherwise much in common. Eulenburg declares: "An infinitely closer figure to de Sade than Rousseau is that Rousseau du ruisseau Rétif de la Bretonne. He was lashed by a powerful sensuality and driven into a kind of exhibitionism by the idolatry of the ego. Therefore he was unequalled in understanding how to analyse the origin, essence and power of sexual life and to devote the ego to a greatly refined worship."

There we have the germs of a literary de Sade but far weaker, more passive and less passionate. Were Rétif more active and impulsive, of a less contemplative nature, and were the means and milieu of the célébré Marquis given to the poor peasant's son from youth onward, then perhaps a second de Sade would have resulted, who would have been literally equal in power and in sensitiveness of description.

Not aimlessly does Rétif praise above all this unusual sensitiveness, this "sensibility, sometimes delicate, sometimes horrible, cruel and wicked." We add to the characteristics of this remarkable writer that he was a passionate connoisseur of women and, unsatisfied with his very numerous mistresses, would run after every pretty girl he met on the street, and would not rest until he had made her acquaintance. He was personally of the greatest uncleanliness. He writes in the Contemporaries: "Since 1773 till today, December 6, 1796, I have brought no new clothes. I have no underwear. An old blue coat is my daily garment." Rétif hence loved cleanliness—in women. He continually spoke thereof, gave detailed information in this connection in his Pornography, and approved the spread of this virtue among the Parisian prostitutes.

Despite his own patient observations he did not hesitate to avail himself of the adventures of others.

Count Alexander of Tilly told in his Memoirs that Rétif de la Bretonne came to him with the request that he tell him his erotic adventures so that he could put them in a book. Very important was the relation of Rétif to Mathieu François Pidanzat de Mairobert (1727-1797), the famous author of The English Spy and the editor of Secret Memoirs of Bachaumont. The latter not only had his works printed at the secret press of Rétif but also collaborated with him in many works. One valuable treatise that appeared from there was Rétif's Pornography on the sixteen classes of prostitutes and panders. Also the Contemporaries, the Owl and the Paternal Malediction were enriched by Pidanzat de Mairobert.

The greatest work of Rétif was undoubtedly Nights of Paris, an inexhaustible thesaurus for the moral life in the Revolutionary period, the only representation of its kind of the moral physiognomy of Paris at the end of the eighteenth century, the true Nocturnal Tableaux of Paris, whose content rendered necessary a twenty years' work. "Every morning," said Rétif, "I wrote down what I had seen in the night." The result was eight voluminous volumes from which unfortunately space does not permit us to quote.

In Monsieur Nicolas (Paris, 1794-1797, 16 vols.) Rétif de la Bretonne told the story of his life more truthfully than the authors of such similar works as Faublas, Clarissa and Heloise. Of especial interest is the thirteenth volume, My Calendar, in which Rétif, day by day, wrote down all the women, whose acquaintance he had made and whom he had seduced and made pregnant.

His Contemporaries is a collection of tales that are founded on actual experiences. The heroes of these adventures were supposed to have authorised the author to use their real names. They are essentially tales of the moral life of the people.

The Farmer and the Perverted Farmer's Wife or the Dangers of the City are the liaisons dangereuses of the lower classes, which preach the sad truth that virtue through constant intercourse with vice necessarily is destroyed.

Fanchette's Feet is the story of a young modist from the Rue Saint-Denis, whose small foot enchanted Rétif, for he was an outspoken foot-fetichist. He had a fanatic passion for pretty women's feet and shoes. Franchette's feet are indeed the heroes of the story.

"Her foot, her small foot, that turns so many heads was shod with a pink pump, so beautifully made and as worthy of enclosing such a beautiful foot that my eyes once fixed on that charming foot could not turn themselves away. Beautiful foot! I said very softly, you don't walk on Persian or Turkish carpets, a beautiful carriage does not guarantee you the fatigue of carrying that superb body, that masterpiece of the graces, but you have an eternal throne in my heart."

He really did see "Franchette" one day in the Rue Saint-Denis, and her feet, "her wonderfully small feet," inspired him to write the story.

The work of Rétif that sounded most like those of the Marquis de Sade was Innocent Saxancour or the Divorced Woman, supposedly the story of his unhappily married daughter, Agnes. Rétif in this work "crossed the boundaries of the boldest cynicism" and the author himself said that one will find in the work "all things that are called atrocities." The unfortunate wife after the marriage had to submit to all the moods of a degenerate roué from her husband; she suffered the most unbelievable infamies and horrors of her passionate tyrant.

We will refer to some other works of his in a later, more pertinent section. In conclusion to our short survey, which stresses only the characteristic works, we wish to remark on two very well known obscene poems of the eighteenth century. The first is Fourtromania, a Lascivious Poem far Connoisseurs. It contained six stanzas, each of 600 verses. The "foutroamania" is the good luck of the gods, that drives away the boredom. But it also makes men happy. The author led the dance of these fortunates with Mlle.

Dubois, an actress of the Comédie Française. Then follow the ladies Aroux and Clarion. At the end of the first stanza appear the duchesses and ladies of the court, who satisfy themselves with their lackeys.

Finally the inexhaustible libido of old Polignac de Paulien is described.

The second stanza starts with the description of the charms of a young girl, who succumbs to the passions of a young roué. Inserted is a poem Father Chrysostome against sexual debaucheries in the convents. Later a man suffering from satyriasis breaks into the convent. Then follows an attack on tribadism and pederasty. The old Due d'Elboeuf was one of the first who introduced the sect of pederasts to France. The conclusion is an excursion on syphilis.

The third stanza is almost entirely devoted to the rôle of syphilis in love. First the high perfection in the healing of this grave ailment is praised; then the "syphilitic heroes of love" are extolled. Archbishop of Lyons, Sire de Montazet, etc., are named together with the Duchesse de Mazarin. After highly indecent expressions on the Duke of Orleans and Madame de Montesson the liaison between the Duchess of Orleans and de l'Aigle as well as de Melfort is disclosed, the last two receiving syphilis from the duchess.

Finally, high praise for Aretino, the discoverer of the "plastic positions."

The fourth stanza is devoted to the praise of the bordellos. The famous procuresses and madantes are presented: Paris, Cardier, Rockingston, Montigny, d'Hericourt and Gourdan. Description of the orgies in these infamous resorts. "Bed and Board" must then follow, hence German women are more susceptible to "foutromania." The author curses Italy where he lost health and wealth.

In the fifth stanza the syphilophobias are encouraged. Not all women have syphilis. Montesquieu had been in the fire as had been Rousseau and Marmontel. Great praise for Dorat, the poète foutromane.

The Hollanders who love only money. Description of the immoral cardinals. Spinola sleeps at Palestrina's, Albani at Altieri's,

Bernis at Saint-Croix, Borghese is… It's too bad that the "Dames de France," the aunts Of Louis XVI, live in celibacy.

Agyroni, the author of a popular work on the therapy of syphilis, is the hero of the sixth stanza. This charlatan had indeed cured the author of his complaint. Numerous medical details as in Robé's poem on syphilis. For a conclusion, "foutromania" is again praised as the soul of the universe.

The second poem, Parapilla, is a translation of the Italian original Il Cazzo (Phallus), the favourite word of Pope Benedict XIV. When a courtier pointed to the obscenity of the word, he replied: "Cazzo, cazzo! I will repeat it until it no longer sounds dirty." The French poem consists of five stanzas whose content, in short, is: Rodric receives from Heaven a certain instrument that makes all women happy. Firstly in Florence, the famous Donna Capponi. Then it thrives in a nunnery in the hands of Lucrezia, the daughter of Alexander VI. The debaucheries of this pope in Rome arc then described and the poem closes with an obscene conversation between him and his daughter.

We could only touch on the most important erotic works of the French literature of the eighteenth century. Their influence on morals was tremendous and the Marquis de Sade was sensible of this influence. In his Ideas on the Novel he showed that he had recognised the significance of pornography. He said: "The epicureanism of Ninon de Lenclos, Marion de Lorme, Marquise de Sévigné and de Lafare, Chaulieu, St. Evremônd, this entire society, tired of mere cytheric love, turned to Buffon, held that only bodily passions were worthwhile in love, and soon changed the style in novels. The writers found it simpler to amuse and corrupt these women than to serve and glorify them. They created incidents, descriptions and conversations more in the spirit of the time and developed its cynicism and immorality in a pleasant, easy and at times philosophic style."

'Marquis de Sade: The Man And His Age, Studies In The History Of The Culture And Morals Of The Eighteenth Century' at Amazon from Magnolia Books.